WIND IN MY HAIR

Following page
Josephine Loewenstein, photographed by Lord Snowdon.

WIND IN MY HAIR

A Kaleidoscope of Memories

Josephine Loewenstein

EDITED BY TOM PERRIN

THE DOVECOTE PRESS

I dedicate this book to my late beloved husband, to
my children and to my grandchildren.
I thank them all for their help and encouragement.

*'Life itself is not the most important thing in life. Some cling to it
as a miser to his money, and to as little purpose. Some risk it for a
song, a hope, a cause, or for wind in their hair.'*

SIR THEODORE FOX
A nineteenth century physician

First published in 2016 by The Dovecote Press Ltd
Stanbridge, Wimborne Minster, Dorset BH21 4JD

ISBN 978-0-9929151-7-9
Text © Josephine Loewenstein 2016
Illustrations © Josephine Loewenstein 2016 (except for those listed
in the Acknowledgements)

Josephine Loewenstein has asserted her rights under the
Copyright, Designs and Patent Act 1988 to be
identified as author of this work

Typeset in Sabon and designed by The Dovecote Press Ltd
Printed and bound in Spain by GraphyCems, Navarra
All papers used by The Dovecote Press are natural, recyclable products
made from wood grown in sustainable, well-managed forests.

A CIP catalogue record for this book is available from the British Library

1 3 5 7 9 8 6 4 2

Contents

Editor's Note

Wind in My Hair started life as a series of short stories written by Princess Josephine Loewenstein throughout her varied and interesting life. These stories, which number more than eighty, have variously been character sketches, accounts of memorable occasions and vignettes of people, places and parties.

More than anything, they have been a means of self-expression for an individual: by putting pen to paper, Josephine Loewenstein has been able to record her feelings and observations. Sometimes this has been in the heat of the moment; at other times it has been with the benefit of hindsight. Either way, she has produced a remarkable patchwork quilt for posterity, a mixture of laughter, sadness, love and the bizarre: all made more colourful by the eccentrics, glamour and celebrity that she has encountered.

Josephine combines a sympathy for and understanding of the human condition with an ability to see the flaws and transience of the various worlds she has inhabited. Her experiences are at once far removed from – and in line with – those of most women of her generation.

In the autumn of 2015, I started to work with Josephine weaving the short stories into a chronological memoir. The text that follows is therefore, entirely Josephine's work. *Wind in My Hair* is rather like a family photograph album: it has been added to throughout the years and occasionally shown to intimates. My role has simply been to help Josephine polish her memories and prepare them for a wider audience.

TOM PERRIN
London 2016

Preface

I hope that this book shows that truth really is stranger than fiction.

JOSEPHINE LOEWENSTEIN
Petersham, September 2016

An old postcard of Church Lane in Ledbury.

ONE

The Years at Ledbury Park

E VERY SUMMER FROM WHEN I WAS BORN I went to Ledbury to stay with my beloved grandparents Jack and Marjorie, Lord and Lady Biddulph.

Ledbury Park was a strange house. It was built in 1590 and was of black and white Tudor architecture. It stood, and still stands, at a busy crossroads in the ancient market town of Ledbury, in Herefordshire. Approximately thirty acres of garden ran uphill alongside a glorious park with fallow deer. All of this was

My maternal grandmother, Marjorie Biddulph.

My grandfather, Jack Biddulph, painted by Philip de László.

not to be seen from the crossroads – or the town – and might not have been there for all you knew. The Biddulph family lived there for 250 years, until my grandfather sold the house in 1949.

Running up the side of the house was the road, which led up to big gates topped with stone lions with shields which opened onto a big cobbled yard, on the left of which there was a lodge. In front of you, on entering the yard, was a long building. This was the laundry and was full of huge hand operated mangles – which were used to wring out the sheets – and other old fashioned paraphernalia. In the courtyard it was very quiet. The front door led into an oak-panelled hall with a highly polished oak wood floor. A grandfather clock ticked peacefully.

The house had been lavishly added onto in the eighteenth and nineteenth centuries. Off the hall was a large dining room. I remember there A. W. Devis's huge painting titled *Lord Cornwallis Receiving the Sons of Tipoo Sahib as Hostages*. Many other family portraits adorned the walls. They were three high on each side. The windows overlooked the garden, which sloped gently up to the ha-ha before the park.

There was a small hall that separated the dining room from the drawing room.

The author as a child.

The walls of this room were lined with white glass fronted bookcases containing my grandparents' considerable collection of eighteenth century china. This was mostly Meissen, Chelsea and Worcester.

The drawing room was formally furnished and I remember two armchairs in particular. They were upholstered in a mauve chintz pattern of ribbons and bows on a cream background. There were large windows over the garden, with wide satin striped brown and cream curtains.

Next, through a double door, was the library. It was rather dark, though it had a high ceiling. They had a valuable collection of books but since then they have been sold and scattered. There were stiff upright chairs covered in striped green and white cotton, known to us as the coffins.

There were log fires in every room, including the bedrooms at night. The cold winters in the war years were unimaginable. All fires were lit but you were only warm standing right up against the mantelpiece.

The tearoom, or oak room as it was called, was the oldest room in the house and felt it too. It looked over the busy street and crossroads, onto which one could peer, through high and small paned windows. At the back was a Victorian conservatory giving over the well of the house. This had stained glass in the dome.

Beyond the oak room the stone passages began. Off these was the servants' hall where the staff ate their meals. If I remember rightly we had a cook, a butler, a housekeeper, my grandmother's ladies maid, a parlour maid, two or three house maids, two scullery maids, three kitchen maids, a boot boy and a butler's boy. There was also Old Chester who looked after the goats. When they sat down to meals they numbered about fifteen.

Along the stone passage was a larder with dark slate surfaces and metal net over the windows, which contained no glass. Food was kept in here as fridges were not known then. Wire cloches were put over the meat and white net over dairy food, butter, cream and milk. Butter was home-made as were all jams and marmalade. Honey was always in the comb.

Further along the passageway was the cook's sitting room, where there always seemed to be a basket of kittens on knitted blankets or old jumpers and a roaring coal fire going. Opposite was the butler's pantry with the silver in tall cupboards. There was a strong metallic smell of the pink paste that they used to clean it with.

Next to the pantry was the scullery and finally the kitchen. This had a large black open range at the end with the words 'Waste Not Want Not' painted on it. The centre of the room was filled by an enormous scrubbed wooden table. Mrs

My governess Foxy sitting with me outside the Old Summer House.

Watson was the cook: she was small and bespectacled and always dressed in a white overall.

Our nursery overlooked the crossroads and was above the oak room. It had a deep windowsill where we could sit and watch the busy street and the cattle going to market. The nannies loved this as it kept us quiet. There was so much going on. The nursery had a fire with a high guard. If we were ever left alone we would put the poker in the fire until it was red-hot and then get a tin of cold water and put it in it. This was rather dangerous but very popular.

We had our meals in the nursery every day except Sunday when my cousin Sebastian and I went on alternate weeks down to lunch in the dining room, where we were allowed half a glass of cider. Herefordshire was cider country and we made a lot of it, including perry that was made of pears. We were allowed this treat when we reached seven or eight years. We had to behave impeccably and talk only when spoken to. If we were sulky or noisy, we were sent away. My grandfather would have no nonsense, silliness or noise.

We were fond of Hawkes the butler. Just before the war the former butler died and there was a great search for a successor. In those days the butlers had to be a certain height. Hawkes fell short of this by a long chalk. They finally decided to waive this rule though it was a great worry at the time. He ended by staying with us for I think about forty years and went to my uncle and aunt at

My cousin Sebastian Yorke with my mother and me at Ledbury.

Underdown at the other end of the park, after my grandparents died. He died in about 1998.

My cousin Sebastian Yorke only lived partly with us during the year, as he went to a friend of his mother's, Lady Diana Worthington, in Buckinghamshire.

We went to separate local schools in Ledbury. I never knew why. I went to Miss Wade and Sebastian went to Miss Ballard. I also had a series of governesses. I was not allowed to cross the road to come home so my governess fetched me after school. All the local school children thought it was my mother – and I did not correct them.

All the summers seemed hot and I ran about in cotton frocks and sandals. We used to go to tea with our cousins at Underdown about once a week. We walked across the park to get there. This took about twenty minutes. My uncle Mike and aunt Amy lived there with their four children, Molly, Susan, Robert and Edward. The house was beautiful. It was an Adam house with rounded façades and windows and a perfect unspoilt view for miles towards Wales. My uncle worked tirelessly in his garden. The weeds were his enemy. Everything was enchantingly planted out with the old rose-coloured brick walls and several

With my cousins Robert, Susan and Molly Biddulph.

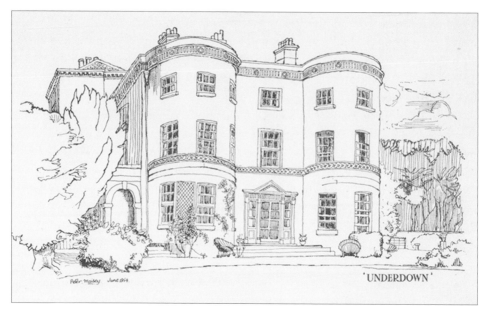

Underdown.

ponds and a walled garden. There was a wonderful parterre with tulips planted amongst forget-me-nots.

Petrol was strictly rationed, and we had little of it. I sometimes bicycled over ten miles to swim or dip in a tiny pool about six feet square in somebody's garden. At one time we kept guinea pigs at the side of a very old thatched cottage which was a summer house half way up the garden. We had all kinds of piebalds and spent a lot of time feeding them and sometimes taking them out into a little wire pen that we put on the lawn.

My mother or my grandmother used to read to me in the evenings before I went to bed. Very often they read books by Mrs Molesworth. *The Tapestry Room* was one of my favourites.

I used to desperately try to prolong the reading as I was terrified of walking up to bed alone. There was a long flight of stairs to go up and endless, long corridors. These were all dimly lit during wartime. I dreaded turning the corners and would finally arrive in my room with my heart thumping. I would wait for my mother to come and say goodnight, but I was still afraid of being left. This was probably largely due to a very vivid imagination.

* * *

Some Christmases before the war we went to my grandfather's house in Kemble near Cirencester. We had no electricity there and I remember going to bed, again along long corridors with a candle and blowing it out when I went to sleep. There was no question of heating in any nursery bedroom, where of course it was most needed.

I was very lonely after my cousins all went to boarding school. I joined them eventually at Lawnside in Great Malvern, which was only twenty minutes away by train. We were hardly allowed visits from parents or family. I was not at all homesick, but it was incredibly cold and uncomfortable.

It was there that I was summoned one evening to the headmistress's study to be told that my father had been seriously wounded in the battle of Monte Cassino in Southern Italy. There was no news of his whereabouts, but it was thought that he had been taken to North Africa, to the American hospital. This was later confirmed. Though I had not seen much of my father due to my parents having separated early in their marriage, I was inordinately upset. On looking back I consider myself lucky. Many girls at that time had to be told that their fathers had died in action.

Once the Second World War started my grandparents had to manage with many less staff. We always kept Hawkes, a Russian cook and, I think, a couple of housemaids. We then moved to the first floor of the house. One of the biggest bedrooms was turned into a drawing room and dining room all in one. The table was in the window with a beautiful view of the garden and park beyond. Fruit was put in rows on the window seat to ripen in the summer.

When I reached a certain age, possibly eight, I was allowed to go into the town alone. There was a brand new Woolworths, which I found extremely exciting. I used to buy a lot of unsuitable things, including a pale pink velvet bow to put on top of my head which I was never allowed to wear. Nothing was over sixpence or a shilling. I saved up my pocket money for those purchases – at Woolworths they also had little painted glass bottles of scent. Each was coloured appropriately. So there was mauve scent for violets and pink for rose. The toy shop was called Tilleys and again was full of treasures of all sorts; soft toys, dolls, dolls houses and furniture – and many books.

The grocery shop was the most old fashioned of all. This was run by a Mr Chadd and his sister Dorrie. He was enormously fat and very good natured. I recall him in a huge leather apron wheezing with laughter. The sister, a spinster, was exceptionally tall and equally smiling. She had sticking out teeth.

Miss Smith kept the sweet shop. She was rather dour but had a nice old mother who helped out. They had lovely striped peppermint balls and tangerine balls and pear drops. Liquorice allsorts are among many other sweets that seem to have died out now.

Sometimes in the summer a Walls ice cream man appeared in the town. In those days this was a cause of great excitement. He arrived on a bicycle with a huge white box on the back. I suppose today this would be a freezer. There were long three cornered water ices in cardboard covers, chocbars and vanilla bars and cornets. These had to be bought out of pocket money.

Occasionally, when we had enough petrol (about every three months), we would take a drive to Cheltenham, Gloucester or Malvern, where we would spend the day. My grandparents had a chauffeur called Richardson, who wore a dark green uniform with breeches and a green cap.

In Cheltenham we always had lunch at the Maison Kunz on the Parade. They served delicious round chocolate shortbread biscuits with a dark chocolate filling. We were allowed only one. We went antique hunting and at that time I saved up my money to buy endless bits of china which my mother advised me about. It was then that I started to build up a knowledge of china and furniture, for which I have to this day a great interest.

Once a year during midsummer gypsies would arrive in the town. They were real Romany gypsies, dark skinned and rather like red Indians with long plaits and ankle length coloured dresses, lots of necklaces and earrings. But the best thing was their caravans. They were wooden and brightly painted in many different colours. And of course they were horse drawn. They had gaudy interiors with carpets and chairs. The children were in long dresses and also wore a lot of jewellery. They invaded the town and went to the market and on Saturday nights they all got extremely drunk and wandered about all night brawling. I remember one woman in particular. She must have been well over six feet tall. She had a tiny head. I was very frightened when I saw her. Anyhow, they usually stayed three or four days, and suddenly the next morning they were gone.

The garden, as I say, sloped gently upwards, and the park with its iron railings was on your right. On the left was a herbaceous border with every kind of brilliant flower imaginable. It was of considerable length and depth. Behind it were tall trees, mostly ilex and running invisibly behind them was a long dark winding path. The gardeners were only allowed to use this path as they were not meant to be visible to anyone walking in the main garden. Of course we preferred this dark mysterious little route. It had a low wall running alongside it and over that was the orchard, which was about four acres.

On either side of the main path going up the garden were tall yew trees cut in the shape of bottles, about eight feet tall each. There was one every few yards.

The garden side of Ledbury Park.

Joe Hillaby writes in *The Book of Ledbury* that the house 'is the grandest black and white house in the country. It dominates and yet is apart from the town with the spacious grounds of Ledbury Park beyond.' My grandfather sold Ledbury in 1949.

With Molly and Susan Biddulph.

Eventually, on the right, there was a beautiful lily pond with an island in the middle. On this island there was a fountain. We played a lot in this pond and bought small boats from Tilleys the toy shop to sail on it.

Next on the right was a pretty and ancient thatched cottage used for storing apples. It was covered in honeysuckle and ivy and there were two large wooden benches either side of the front door painted yellow. In front of the cottage was a grass tennis court.

Looking across the park you could see Bowling Green Cottage – this was actually quite a big house – which my grandparents let to their friends, Lord and Lady Ruthven for the duration of the war. Lord Ruthven was good looking. He was tall with white hair and had a perfect figure. He used to say that one must always leave the table hungry. His wife was very fat and unwieldy. He was head of the Home Guard in Ledbury. It was more like *Dad's Army* than you can possibly imagine. The Ruthvens had a beautiful old maroon car. He did the steering and she operated the gears.

Further up the garden was a gentian bed – they grew particularly well in our red Herefordshire earth. This was in front of the gate to the kitchen garden. This was some three acres in size and had large green houses at the top end.

There were peaches on the walls, nectarines and apricots and all kinds of vegetables. Beyond it we had a flower bed each, to grow what we liked. There was a further lily pond. This one did not have an island. I fell into it once and was heavily dosed with cod liver oil, in case I had swallowed any of the water.

When you reached the top of the garden there was a summer house perched up above with a spectacular view for hundreds of miles. Just below it was the head gardener's cottage. He was called Mr Bishop. You could sit on the terrace of this summer house on benches and inside was a display of majolica china on shelves, and also a big table.

Beyond, higher up, the wood started. It was dense and there were several ancient cottages standing in clearings that you came across unexpectedly. The wood spread above the park to Underdown and beyond.

In those days food was rationed. First throughout the war, and then for some years afterwards. When my Uncle Mike came over to tea we could see him striding over the park from the dining room window. We had to hide our rations as he would otherwise eat them on sight and we would be left with nothing.

I remember walking with my Aunt Dig, past the ripe peaches, one day during the Second World War.

'How sad it is that we cannot enjoy the peaches now,' she said to me.

'Why ever not?' I responded.

'Because there is nobody to pick them,' she said.

TWO

A Portrait of My Mother

I PARKED MY CAR in a small Chelsea street of doll like houses. My mother lived in one of these houses. Her front door was dark green and had a thin number shakily painted onto it. She had painted this herself.

The weather was blustery and it was raining hard. I stood on the doorstep waiting. I realised that I was early and was debating in my mind whether or not to ring the bell. I weighed up my options and thought that for once I would risk it. The appointment for tea was for five o'clock – and it was seven minutes to, after all. I pushed the bell, and as I did so, I heard my mother's voice in my head: 'You must never be late and never be early.'

My mother's house, 39 Bury Walk.

Above left: My mother as a child with my grandmother.

Above right: A press photograph of my mother from the 1920s.

There was no answer.

I rang several more times and then gave up and went to sit in the car. My temper was rising.

I waited until five minutes past and returned to the house. The door was answered immediately.

'Oh, there you are,' said my mother. 'You're a bit late.'

I replied that I had rung several times just before five o'clock.

'Well, I wasn't ready,' she snapped. 'And you know it's rude to arrive early.'

* * *

Throughout my lonely childhood I had learnt not to argue with my mother as it courted danger and was useless.

Mary Lowry-Corry had been a great beauty. And on that day that I went for tea with her, this was still evident. She had wonderfully large sapphire eyes and a delicately wrought face. Decades of admiration and adulation had made her spoilt and capricious. Her figure and legs had been perfect but she was now too thin. She was witty, thoroughly original, fanciful and at times brilliantly

My father in the uniform of the Grenadier Guards aged nineteen.

Dromoland Castle, Co. Clare, the O'Brien stronghold. It is now a hotel.

amusing, especially when she chose to mimic. She had been born Mary Constance Biddulph, in 1906. She was the second daughter of my grandparents and was educated at home with governesses, later going to a school in South Kensington with a purple uniform.

In 1929 she had married my father, Montagu Lowry-Corry. It was considered a suitable marriage and I think that they were both persuaded into it by their respective families. They were young and beautiful.

My father was a cousin of the Northern Irish family of the Earls of Belmore and his mother was a daughter of Lord Inchiquin of Dromoland Castle, Co. Clare: Southern Irish but Protestant since the time of Queen Elizabeth I. My father was heir to a considerable fortune and estates descending from his great uncle, Lord Rowton, who had been a close friend of Queen Victoria and private secretary to the Victorian Prime Minister, Benjamin Disraeli.

As a child, I did see many of my father's family, especially my Paget cousins, David and Rosalind. Their mother, my aunt Rosemary, had decided on a career as an actress before the war. My grandmother (her stepmother) had been horrified and refused to give her a coming out ball. Luckily she married one of the kindest and most charming men I have ever known. Arthur Paget was a son of Minnie Stevens, one of the great American heiresses of the nineteenth century. He was a truly kind

MARRIAGE ANNOUNCEMENTS

Mr. Montagu W. Lowry-Corry and the Hon. Mary Biddulph

The engagement is announced of Montagu William Lowry-Corry, Grenadier Guards, only son of Brigadier-General Noel Lowry-Corry and the Hon. Mrs. Lowry-Corry, and Mary, younger daughter of Lord and Lady Biddulph.

My parents' engagement is announced.

My parents' wedding at The Guards' Chapel in 1929.

Minnie Stevens.

Queen Mary.

and loving uncle to me and I will never forget him. They lived in Bryanston Square in a big house with many servants and also in a very pretty house in Kent.

At this time my uncle was equerry to Queen Mary. When in waiting he had to sleep at Buckingham Palace overnight. As nothing much ever happened my uncle once decided to go to the theatre. That happened to be the night the Crystal Palace burnt down. The Queen expressed a wish to go and see this.

'Where is my gentleman?' she said.

She was unable to go without him.

But alas, my parents, except from a point of view of class, were never compatible – and their marriage only lasted a short time.

I was born in 1931 at their home in Chelsea. I hardly remember my father from my early childhood as he separated from my mother when I was about three years old. They divorced not long afterwards.

After my parents divorced, my mother became rather short of money. Accordingly, we lived in rather tough conditions. We had no central heating in our house, only occasional electric bar fires. When we needed hot water, we had

My christening in Chelsea, 1931.

to stoke the boiler, bringing buckets of coal from the cellar into the house. We could not afford to decorate the house. We used to listen to the war news on a small Bakelite radio but then one day this burst into flames and had to be thrown away. There was no question of replacing it.

My mother could not cook and so often we went out for a cheap lunch at a local Greek restaurant called 'The Unity'. The menu was relentless: always fish and chips, omelette and chips or some unknown meat and chips. There was quite a lot of horsemeat around at that time and so there may have been some of that too. From time to time I would go to my father's grand flat in Bayswater for a proper tea, but otherwise I became quite undernourished. But nobody seemed to notice. I think that this might have helped to cause my present severe osteoporosis.

When I started to earn some money, my mother forbad me from contributing to the housekeeping. Instead she encouraged me to save up for something of my own. And so I saved up £60 and bought my first piano: an upright Broadwood. It is still going strong and I play on it each morning to this day, saving my Steinway for practice in the evening and for concerts, which we hold about four times each year.

My parents walking in Hyde Park shortly before their divorce.

A portrait of my mother by Adrian Daintrey.

* * *

When I was invited to my mother's house, she always took great trouble over the tea. Little individual tables were placed next to the armchairs and I was always given the tea that I liked (very strong Typhoo) along with hot scones or croissants, cakes and chocolate biscuits.

The room was pretty but shabby. There were pieces of valuable early Chelsea china dotted about it and a good upright French bureau with lots of little drawers. Various photographs of her adored grandchildren were to be seen. There were some good mirrors and furniture but the curtains were in tatters. The springs in nearly all of the chairs were broken.

On the whole I enjoyed these teas. There was an old-fashioned feel about them. It was always an unhurried event full of interesting conversation and often some gossip.

My mother would have many hilarious stories of rows in the shops, and scenes on the buses (she only took public transport). Every conductor, passenger and shop assistant would be brilliantly imitated.

That day, I rose to go to the bathroom.

'Now don't pull the chain too hard or I'll never get it right again,' she said.

'I know, I know,' I replied, exasperated.

On the landing floor, I noticed a small jug of cream.

'Whatever is that doing there?' I asked her.

'Well, there's a draught. So it's there to keep it cool, of course.'

My mother would have no machinery in the house in case it broke down. So there was no fridge, radio, Hoover, toaster, electric kettle or television. This presented quite a few problems and meant that shopping had to be done practically daily.

'Just pop down to the kitchen darling and get the sugar on your way back will you,' she called out as I left the room.

Afterwards, I descended to the kitchen. There, I saw a large clacking alarm clock standing on the floor against a hole in the wainscoting. The hands were motionless.

By this time, nothing that my mother did surprised me.

'What on earth is that clock doing down there on the floor?' I asked, after having slumped back into the broken armchair.

'There was a mouse in the kitchen so I put that old clock in front of its hole. Anyway it has worked wonderfully well.'

'Why don't you put a trap down, like anyone else?'

'Oh dear no, that would be terribly creepy and anyhow, what would I do with it afterwards?'

* * *

When I lived with my mother in Royal Avenue in Chelsea as a child, after the war, she was always interviewing for new help for the house. I usually tried to stay out of the way as I found the whole ordeal agonising, always knowing that, even if she engaged someone, they would be gone in two or three days. It was always a cook-housekeeper that was needed: in other words, a body.

I remember arriving home after one interview.

'How did it go?' I asked.

'Well,' my mother replied. 'She seemed fairly alright. But then came the rejoinder: 'Except she had cigarette ash on her hat.'

We had a daily for quite a long time whom my mother adored. She was very plump and pretty and reliable. But then, one day, we had a burglary. When the daily arrived the next morning my mother broke the news to her. She promptly fainted away and we had to lay her out on the sofa and fan her and make her strong tea. My mother was furious.

So that was the end of her.

* * *

On the whole the neighbours were reviled and despised by my mother, but nevertheless minutely observed.

My mother said one day, 'I saw the Commander lying in bed in his basement today, he waved a skinny arm as I walked by. I hope he's not ill.'

'Well did you ring the bell and ask?'

'Of course not. He's got a perfectly good sister like a Sergeant Major.'

'But how do you know she's there?'

'Well I don't. Anyway I can't help that,' she responded snappily.

Another time, my mother tripped and fell into the gutter on the street. Being in some pain she did not immediately get up. A couple of neighbours walked straight by. She told me about this a few days later.

'How awful!' I cried. 'Didn't they help you up?'

'Oh no,' she responded briskly, 'why should they? I wouldn't have helped them if they had fallen down.'

* * *

The summer of 1976 was extraordinarily hot. I spent most of it in a cottage I had persuaded my husband to buy – against his will – recovering from various illnesses. I talked often to my mother on the telephone. We puzzled about the really intense heat. It was late August, then September and still ninety degrees, even early in the morning. There was a strange mist and the sun regularly rose, like a huge red ball. The ground was yellow with drought. I thought it was all rather exciting, as I particularly enjoy extremes of climate.

'I know what it is!' my mother said, suddenly ringing one morning.

'What is it?' I replied.

'It's all those coloured people we have over here now. The sun has just followed them. Funny, I didn't think of it before. That's quite clear.'

I shrieked with laughter, but she was serious and wrote a letter to *Country Life* on the subject. Unfortunately it was not published.

* * *

The great love of my mother's life was Goronwy Rees: a brilliant, good-looking homme fatale. He was a Fellow of All Souls and was at one time mooted to be one of the notorious spies at the time of Kim Philby's defection to Russia. This was never proven however. During the war he often came to Ledbury to stay with us when he was on leave from the army. He used to take Sebastian and me to a little café above Tilley's to have ginger beer which was in stone bottles. We made a lot of noise blowing down straws to make bubbles and giggle uncontrollably. Goronwy just smiled and chatted on to my mother.

* * *

Somehow the little house in Chelsea was a magnet for burglars. Over the years, at fairly regular intervals I would get a desperate telephone call.

'Oh, dear it's so awful,' my mother called one day, sobbing.

'I've just got back and found everything strewn all over the place. Mother's table has gone and I don't know what else. You must come quickly.'

'Have you rung the police?'

'Not yet.'

(She was still sobbing).

'Now don't worry, I'll come round at once.'

I leapt into my car and drove like the wind to Chelsea. I arrived to find my mother on the doorstep with a huge policeman beside her. He was tall and fat. The front door had accidentally slammed and of course the keys were left inside. The small Georgian window by the front door was slightly open.

'Now,' said my mother to the policeman, 'you ought to be able to open that window and get in but you're so overweight it's a disgrace. You had better go back to the police station and get someone else.'

'Well madam,' he responded, a bit shamefaced, 'I can't do that.'

'I'd better get in myself then,' she said briskly.

And so she climbed on the railing quick as a flash and got through the window, opening the front door triumphantly.

Her younger grandson rang later to commiserate.

'Yes, it was all terrible darling,' she said to him, 'but so exciting.'

My mother had no burglar alarm because that came into the category of machinery. When she went away, on leaving, she would stand back from the house and call out 'Goodbye, goodbye!' and wave up at the window, even if there was no one about to see.

* * *

Shopping was a great activity for my mother; she had a passion for it. Mostly, she would not buy anything but would closely observe the assistants and customers and above all, the goods.

Once she was in Harrods at the glove counter. An anaemic young lady was serving her.

'I would like to see some fabric gloves,' she said.

'What colour Madam?'

'Mid-stone,' she replied.

There was a pause.

'Do you mean fawn Madam?'

'No, I do not mean fawn, I said mid-stone.'

(By now she was getting ratty).

The girl turned and looked bleakly into row after row of glass drawers and finally pulled out a pair of dark brown gloves.

'But those are n****r brown,' my mother said to her furiously.

'Madam, you can't say that nowadays,' the young lady exclaimed.

She was clearly shocked.

My mother and I with the boys at Bury Walk.

'I'll say what I like,' retorted my mother.

The girl stepped between the counters to search again. Her irate customer noticed that she had no shoes on and was in stockinged feet.

I'll have to report that to the manager, she thought.

And so, after some enquiries she sailed up in the lift to the fifth floor 'Customer Complaints Office'. There, in a wheelchair, she found a charming and deeply sympathetic middle aged woman, who was clearly highly trained for the job. She too was duly shocked and horrified by my mother's revelation – and so the two ladies spent a long time discussing every aspect of the shoeless assistant.

My mother returned home, and was thoroughly satisfied with her sortie to Harrods. It was all to be mulled over later, with me on the telephone.

* * *

My mother had an absolute horror of disabilities of any kind.

When we once had a cocktail party at our home in Chelsea, two of our friends entered the room together. One was crippled and had a heavy limp and the other was tall and looked rather like a walking corpse. At the moment that these two men entered the room, my mother rose immediately and left the room and the house.

One year, while staying with a friend in Venice with Nancy Mitford, an intellectual friend who was wheelchair bound was also a guest. Towards the end of our stay, I asked Nancy if she was enjoying the holiday.

'No,' she replied, continuing that it was the limit to have someone disabled to stay and that it had ruined her holiday.

Later, my mother and she conferred over the incident together.

'Thoroughly creepy and tiresome,' was my mother's verdict, which Nancy most certainly agreed with.

* * *

One winter we went to my sons' concert at their public school. They were both playing in the orchestra. It was slippery and dark when we went out to get some air in the interval. All of a sudden, my mother slipped and fell heavily. It was extremely painful for her but she protested that she was quite alright. She got through the rest of the evening on sheer willpower.

She spent a long time in bed in the little Chelsea house after that. She had obviously broken her hip. But she would not see the doctor.

As it was the boys' holiday they were in attendance. She used to lower a small basket on a rope with the shopping list and money in it.

In general it was her habit to buy half a cucumber and cut it up and add salt, instead of bothering with salad. She would usually eat this with some chicken. The younger grandson was a clever boy, and he actually found a miniature cucumber in a shop, as the supermarket had run out of half cucumbers. She looked doubtfully and with some irritation at this.

'Is it not acceptable?' he asked.

'No,' she replied. 'It's so kind of you darling, but I would rather have my usual half.'

As my mother could not get out to cash a cheque, I brought in some pound notes now and then. Never more than ten at a time were accepted.

One particular time my mother was carefully counting the notes and, low and behold, she suddenly caught sight of a Scottish pound note. She let out a shout of outraged irritation.

'How tiresome, surely you could have noticed it?' she said.

'Well I didn't,' I replied.

(I was actually very tired at the time as my daughter was still very young. She had been left with the daily for an hour.)

'You will have to go back and change it.'

'Well I can't now, I've got to get back to give Dora her tea. I'll do it tomorrow morning.'

'No, you must go at once. I can't bear it.'

I looked at my mother and realised that the Scottish pound note was a sort of equivalent of a wild beast to her. I was too tired to argue and so slogged off back to the bank to change it.

* * *

My mother enjoyed sports, particularly playing tennis. She was an intrepid rider and often rode to hounds in her youth.

In the late 1980s we went to one of her childhood homes, Kemble, to look around.

'Let's just look and see if my old groom Lewis is still alive,' my mother said to me.

So, we went down a little narrow lane, towards his cottage. We knocked on the door and lo' and behold, there he was. He was a small and wiry man, wearing a flat cap and a spotty handkerchief, tied around his neck. He was thrilled to see my mother.

'She used to go like the wind out hunting!' he exclaimed.

He must have been in his nineties by then and his cottage was tiny. It was very bare, had a small iron grate and a little wooden table covered with newspaper, where he ate his lunch. A neighbour prepared this for him.

My mother was clearly delighted to see him. I think that, for her, it was an important experience: in her old age, it reminded her of her childhood and all of those people and places that had long since gone.

* * *

After spending Christmas 1991 with us, my mother went home and we went down to stay at Badminton for New Year. As usual, I rang her several times but as she was deaf I was not surprised that there was no answer. After the weekend, I rang again, but there was still no answer.

I got on my coat and was just setting off for Chelsea when the door bell rang. I opened it to find a particularly young policeman standing there, hat in hand. I knew at once what had happened.

'Could I come in a moment and speak to you Madam?' he asked politely.

I took him into the drawing room.

And then came the inevitable words: 'you better sit down.'

My mother had been found dead, fallen up her staircase, he told me. Burglars had entered and stolen a French commode, leaving the front door open. This was all rather gruesome and shocking. I told him to fetch my husband from the library, where he was with his secretary.

'But will you be all right if I leave the room?' he asked.

He was very kind and it was obvious that it was the first time he had had to impart such news.

My mother's house was cordoned off by the police for several days, whilst the front door was mended, the locks were changed and everything was looked into.

We had the funeral and burial at Kemble, which was her favourite childhood home.

Grief for a parent is a strange thing and I found afterwards that bouts of weeping came on at unexpected times for months. I felt rather as if I had had a limb amputated or had lost a part of my body.

THREE

The Ballet

M Y LIFE CHANGED SIGNIFICANTLY WHEN I WAS THIRTEEN. The war was drawing to a close. In one of the holidays I caught chickenpox. My mother decided to move back up to London – even though the bombing was not yet completely over – so that I could recuperate. Though she was becoming bored by life in the country and the tedium of her war work with my aunt Amy Biddulph in Great Malvern, she did enjoy meeting and spending time with the phalanx of

My aunt Amy Biddulph.

dashing Belgian and French officers that they met and became friends with.

So she found us a house in Chelsea, in Royal Avenue. Property was then cheap there.

Shortly after moving in, I fell ill again, this time with measles. I was delirious for several days. When I made a full recovery, I persuaded my mother to arrange for me to have an audition with Ninette de Valois, the director of the Sadler's Wells Ballet, the precursor to the Royal Ballet.

I had decided at the age of six or seven that I wanted to have a career in ballet. This was the result of being taken to see Colonel de Basil's Ballets Russes at Covent Garden. The three so-called 'Baby Ballerinas', Tamara Toumanova, Tatiana Riabouchinska and Irina Baronova, who had been discovered in their very early teens by George Balanchine, were all the rage at the time. My cousin Sebastian came with me, armed with his scout knife. I asked him whether he had enjoyed the performance. He replied, 'No, because nobody fell over.'

At Ledbury, in the holidays, I had attended Miss Dovey's dancing classes, which were a mix of classical ballet and ballroom dancing. She gave displays in the local drill hall, which I performed in.

At one point Miss Dovey was short of a pianist for the classes. My mother recommended a replacement called Mr Griffiths. I had, and still have, no idea where she found him. He had an extremely sinister aspect and wore a belted overcoat and a homburg hat, which he pulled down low over thick glasses. He smelt strongly of a rheumatic medicine in vogue at the time. Miss Dovey did not like the look of him at all, but my mother was adamant that he would do. Anyhow, he lasted only a few weeks before he was arrested and tried (and, given the times, probably hanged) for shooting his boyfriend dead. This was a major scandal. Miss Dovey was furious and said to my mother, 'I told you so,' on at least one occasion.

Despite this drama, I managed to progress in my dancing and the audition at the New Theatre near Trafalgar Square went well. I was accepted by Ninette de Valois into the Sadler's Wells School.

This also presented a dilemma however, as it meant leaving school. Of course I did not mind, but I think that my mother felt guilty about this. But she gave in finally. She loved the arts in any form and was delighted to be back in London. Though the rockets, or 'doodle bugs' as they were called, were falling around us, they did not concern me at all.

I started in the ballet school the following year, when I was aged fourteen. It was hard at first as the classes were far more advanced than at Miss Dovey's and it took me a while to catch up. We saw quite a few of the stars, including Margot

Self (on the right) in class at the Sadler's Wells Theatre in 1945.

Fonteyn and Moira Shearer, who had begun to film the *Red Shoes* with Léonide Massine – she used to make up and dress at the theatre and then get into a taxi to go to the filming.

Sometimes these magical creatures would join our classes. At the age of fourteen or fifteen, it was dazzling to be working alongside them: we would all do the same thing at the barre and concentrate on the same exercises but then

Dancing in *Turandot*, top right.

later there would be a chance to watch the stars when dance arrangements or enchainments were practised in the middle of the floor.

Moira Shearer was ethereal, thin and beautiful to look at. I was never a great admirer of her as a dancer though. I always preferred the Russian dancers. My first glimpse of Margot Fonteyn was as she went through the stage door at the Sadler's Wells Theatre. I remember thinking how pretty she was, in her mid-twenties, with her black hair setting off beautiful white flower earrings.

We students did not mix with the stars socially. There was a natural distance. But they were always kind to us – we were only children, after all. Margot Fonteyn was very friendly; I got to know her socially much later, after I was married.

Training to be a dancer is certainly hard, and when you begin to perform, very much harder. It is a completely enclosed life with no time whatever to do anything else. The move into Covent Garden had not yet taken place and so we had no fixed rehearsal rooms and would find ourselves in various rented premises. The day before we would check on the board to see where and when we had to turn up.

The journey to the theatre from Chelsea took about an hour and a half every morning. On the 22 bus I left home at eight o'clock. The bus took me to the stage door of the Sadler's Wells Theatre in Islington. We started with an ordinary daily class at half past nine. This was followed throughout the day by mime and character classes, where we would work on folk dances like the mazurka or the csardas.

The boys group joined us at the later classes to partner us. Kenneth Macmillan was studying there then alongside John Cranko and David Blair, both of whom I danced with. The boys were a bit on the rough side. Macmillan showed no particular sign at the time of the great choreographer that he would later become: indeed he was not a particularly good dancer.

During the classes, Ninette de Valois would arrive unannounced. Everyone was petrified of her. And with reason. She was small, good-looking and had beautiful eyes. She was a formidable force. She would come into the class, look around and say, 'Who's the girl on the right there?' Then, those eyes might scan the room and settle on you. 'Come here,' she would say. And then she would make you repeat the step. You never knew what was going to happen next.

Although the dancing was wonderful, the discipline was rigid. There was no cheekiness. You were kept absolutely in your place. We were extremely obedient and modest. And when it came to the allocation of parts, the process was ruthless. They would try you out, reject you and choose someone else. No one took your feelings into consideration, which was hard to stomach when you were young.

When I was fifteen, the opening of Covent Garden Opera House with a production of *Sleeping Beauty* was being planned. It was to be a grand gala with the King and Queen and the Princesses Elizabeth and Margaret attending – with everyone in white tie and wearing decorations. Rumours whirled about that some of us might be chosen to perform, walk on or have dancing parts. We waited with great trepidation for the notices to go up on the board.

IN THE ROYAL BOX AT COVENT GARDEN : The King and Queen, Queen Mary, Princess Elizabeth and Princess Margaret watching "The Sleeping Beauty." The Queen wore a picture dress of plain grey tulle ornamented with rows of cyclamen and silver and scalloped embroidery. With it she wore a small tiara of diamonds. Both Princesses had sprays of white flowers at the shoulder

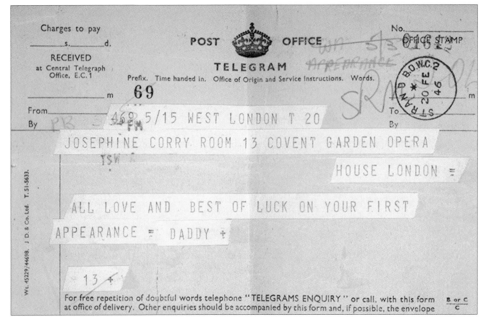

A telegram from my father.

At last the day came. As far as I can remember, about twenty of us were chosen to play the parts of court ladies, peasants, witches, rats and mice. The excitement was absolutely overwhelming. But I did feel so sad for those that were not chosen.

Fittings for costumes and rehearsals began at once. The Opera House was redecorated and underwent a complete renovation, as it had been a dance hall during the war. Oliver Messel designed the costumes and sets. I knew him before through my mother's family. I never met a sweeter, kinder or more patient man. He was always polite to everyone, tactful and good-natured. This was unusual in the theatre. When Colin Tennant developed the island of Mustique, he asked Oliver to design the first houses.

Money was scarce and we were put to work sewing some of the costumes that Messel designed. Everyone had to muck in. Margot Fonteyn's mother, Mrs Hookham, was in charge of making sure the dressmaking work was completed. I found her sharp and intolerant. She was one of the most unpleasant people I have ever met. She was totally driven. Margot was like a puppet in her mother's hands.

One day I was sewing the ermine tails on to the king's cloak. I sewed them all the way round through ignorance. I remember Mrs Hookham being furious. I had to undo them all and start again, which took days.

The great gala loomed. It was to take place in January 1946. Things became tense: everything had to be perfect and ready in time. We attended endless fittings and each day was highly organised. It felt like being in an army before battle. One was always being told what to do and there were always list of tasks for each day: a fitting at nine o'clock here, a rehearsal at four o'clock there. It was non-stop all day. We had no chance to go home between the various commitments and had to grab a quick sandwich for lunch, with spreads from little glass pots. But there was hardly any time to eat.

My mother and father had decided to get two tickets and put up with each other just for that one night. The evening all passed in rather a haze.

* * *

In 1947, it was announced that the Covent Garden Opera was to tour the provinces and that some famous international singers would travel with them and take part. Six of the Sadler's Wells Ballet School students had been chosen to dance in various productions since the opening of the Opera House the previous January. We eagerly awaited the announcement on the notice board of who was to go on the first tour since the war.

There were six places, to dance in *Rigoletto*, *Carmen* and *Turandot* which were among the six or eight operas to be performed. The choreography for *Rigoletto* was written for us by John Cranko, later to become well known in his field. We also had to take lessons in Spanish dancing for *Carmen*. The tour was to be two months long. I was lucky enough to be chosen and was delirious with excitement, which was only tempered by the fact that I knew that I had to persuade my mother to let me go. I realized that this would be well nigh impossible. My best friend, later to be a soloist in the ballet company, was also chosen. We carefully thought out how to word the news and how to persuade our parents.

At the outset my mother refused point blank. I think that if I had been her I would have done the same. We were all barely sixteen. Times were hard, and food was scarce: in fact it was still rationed. Polio and diphtheria were rife. No one had any money and we had very few clothes. We told a good many white lies to persuade them, amongst which for example, that Ninette de Valois had said that the experience would be invaluable for us. Finally, at the eleventh hour, they capitulated. We were to be chaperoned by a red-faced stage manager called Robby.

It was one of the hottest summers in living memory. We set off in the middle of August from St Pancras Station. My friend and I quickly plucked another girl,

During the Covent Garden Opera tour.

Baritono **PAOLO SILVERI**

The great baritone!

whom we quite liked, from the other four so that we would be two groups of three. Two separate lodging houses in each city were arranged. The company was, I suppose, about two hundred strong. The chorus was mostly Welsh.

My mother and some of the other girls' parents saw us off. Lots of instructions and dire warnings were given, to which we barely listened. It was freedom at last.

The train was unbearably hot. We wandered about the corridors with wolf whistles following us from the men's chorus. Paolo Silveri, the Italian baritone, was on board, a handsome swarthy type whom I had already fallen in love with (not that I knew him) at Covent Garden earlier in the year. His presence was part of the reason why I was so determined to go on the tour. My mother had not known this, and luckily had not seen him on the platform. I only admired him from a distance and vice versa. He had a large fair lady with him in a hat. She turned out to be his wife, so my friends had to console me. It was a long journey to Glasgow, which was the first city we were going to. It took all day and was dark when we got there.

A programme from the opera tour.

Unbeknown to me, my mother had contacted a cousin of mine, called Cicely. She was aged about fifty and had been asked to check out our lodgings. She was a hearty type with a bellowing voice: she dressed in tweeds and brogues and always had a brace of dogs on a lead with her. I was mortified as everyone turned round and stared incredulously as she marched briskly up towards us on the platform. It turned out that there had been a muddle about the 'digs' and that we had nowhere to go. Cousin Cicely had booked us in to the Y.W.C.A. I thanked her profusely, but winced as she roared about. She directed us to the address and then luckily left, never bothering us again. I was much teased, needless to say.

We changed to our digs the next day. They were typical show business lodgings: the landlady was inquisitive, the rooms were stuffy, the curtains were made of lace and most girls had to share beds. Luckily I had a single bed. Our late meal after the theatre was tea and scones and occasionally a little cold meat – often spam as I remember.

We rehearsed quite a bit during the day, so I was able to see the baritone at close quarters. He was singing *Rigoletto*, Count de Luna in *Trovatore* and alternating with another English baritone (with whom my friend had fallen in love) as the toreador in *Carmen*. We found all this exciting and romantic. The third member of our little group was being hotly pursued by the stage manager whom she later married.

When we were not performing we stood in the wings and watched the other performances, which taught us a lot, and laid the foundations for our love of opera. We also had the luck of hearing the great soprano, Eva Turner, who travelled up from London for the performances of *Turandot*. We had danced in this at Covent Garden earlier in the season. The rehearsals with her were an ordeal. She was a perfectionist and nothing was ever right.

The principal scene was set on a vast staircase filling the whole stage. We had to bear her train, three on each side. Timing was vital according to how she moved about during the famous aria, 'In questa regia'. The train was immensely heavy. We had to walk up and down the staircase and then sit neatly down, all at the same time, when she stopped moving. This was easier said than done and we were constantly yelled at and upbraided. In the end we got the knack of it and she was a little pleasanter.

After two weeks we left for Liverpool, where our digs were next-door to the theatre, so that we could walk home at night instead of taking the tram. Again it was only buns and tea after the show.

In Manchester I fell ill. The landlady feared that I had caught polio and so did not come near me or bring me anything to eat. I had a fever, which was probably brought on by tiredness or excitement. The girls brought me a lettuce roll after rehearsals at about four p.m. My old governess Foxy came to visit me. She was always good natured but was essentially a very vague person. She did not really seem to notice that I was in bed. Anyhow, in the report that she gave my mother she said that I couldn't have been in better form. I recovered in a day or two.

We then went on to Birmingham, where we bought ourselves little metal bracelets with the names of our various loves engraved on them. By this point, the tour was drawing to a close. The last stage was Croydon, which we had to reach from home on a long and complicated journey. When our freedom was gone, we were like horses back in their stables.

* * *

On arriving at Covent Garden backstage one morning I paused in front of the notice board and saw (miracle of miracles) that I was called to rehearsals for the *Boutique Fantasque,* for the part of one of the two spinsters. It was to be directed and danced by Léonide Massine and Moira Shearer was to be the principle ballerina. My excitement knew absolutely no bounds. Massine had been one of Diaghilev's great discoveries and had taken Nijinsky's place when he had retired due to mental illness. He had also danced with the Colonel de Basil Company before the war. Massine was always a romantic figure to me: dark and mysterious.

The rehearsals were a wonderful experience and enabled me to see this great dancer at work. He had an even temperament, was unfailingly courteous and sensitive, and cared for us all. He was a wonderful teacher and patiently explained the ballet in such an inspired and gentle way that it was totally comprehensible. No shouting was required.

The sets were also delightful and André Derain, who originally designed them, came to rehearsals. I first saw him standing stock still in the middle of the stage at Covent Garden in a hat and a huge belted overcoat (he was a colossal man) with a small bespectacled girl assistant beside him holding a clipboard.

This was followed by a part in *Giselle* and some extra work with the New York City Ballet in the summer, at that time led by André Eglevsky, Rosella Hightower and Nora Kaye. The dancers were dynamic and virile, compared to the standards of our company. They were technically far ahead.

After this the school moved for a short time to Chalk Farm, then to Barons Court. It was at this time that I met the girl who was to become the closest friend in my life. Mary Drage was a beautiful and talented dancer, who rose to become a soloist in the ballet company. We have now been friends for seventy years.

Mary Drage, my ballet friend, marries Rory Fraser.

It was then that I finally realised that I would have to leave the school as I was too tall for classical ballet and would not be able to progress further. There was a height limit of five foot six inches. It was something that was devastating to come to terms with. I had been warned of this during my original interview with Ninette de Valois. She had thought that I was older than twelve, as I was quite tall for my age.

Although I must have been aware of the possibility that I might grow too tall, I had put it to the back of my mind.

But then, one day, the Principal of the school sent for my mother and told her that I was too tall and that she did not think it would benefit me to stay on longer (although they did allow me to have one last term). I went into a great depression. My mother was exceptionally kind and tried everything that she could to comfort me.

After I left Sadler's Wells, I used to go to public ballet classes run by Vera Volkova near Leicester Square. Here, one saw all the leading ballet dancers and people from show business. It was there that I got to know Audrey Hepburn, who was looking for work at the time. I was asked to audition for *Cinderella* at the Palladium, where they had engaged Pauline Grant, formerly a classical dancer, who had became a choreographer. They had decided to have a classical ballet inserted into the Cinderella story and were looking for ballet dancers. I signed a contract for three months.

It was gruelling work but quite well paid. We had nine changes of costume in each show and two shows daily, from noon until eleven o'clock at night, every day except Sunday. Pauline Grant was a hard and exacting ballet mistress and we had endless rehearsals, often into the night and at various far flung locations. And of course there were rehearsals throughout the run of the show.

The stars were Evelyn Laye, Tommy Trinder and Roma Beaumont. I also met a dancer who became one of my closest friends. Diane Bessel was half Russian and her father's family were the original publishers of Mussorgsky's *Boris Godunov*. Alas she died in 2014. Her family were kind to me and her mother was extraordinarily motherly, a charming and delightful person, as indeed was her father. They lived in a house that formerly belonged to Lily Langtry in Earl's Court Square.

After the Palladium show was over, I decided to give up dancing since I did not want to continue a career in musical shows, which were meaningless to me. I didn't want to be a showgirl.

In 1948 my aunt Rosie Paget and my father gave a coming out ball for my cousin Rosalind and me. In addition I had to do the season and go to all the other debutante balls, Ascot and the Buckingham Palace garden party. I fought against this as I was still in the throes of theatre life and could not bear to miss out on it.

Somehow or other I managed both. I was asked to be debutante of the year and to be photographed by Cecil Beaton. This I refused as no one in the ballet world knew of my other life and I would have been mortified if they had. Also I was still madly in love with the Italian opera singer from the tour. Though nothing could come of that of course.

After I started this new life I really did not enjoy it much and missed the theatre terribly. I suppose I behaved rather selfishly, as my father had made a great effort for me. He had bought a house in Bembridge on the Isle of Wight, where we sailed a lot and had friends to stay.

After two or three years, a young man friend (not a boyfriend) said to me that he was going to Rome for twelve days, as he was separating from his girlfriend.

'Why not come along?' he suggested.

So we travelled together. I was thrilled by the idea and told my father I was going for just a few days.

He wasn't worried. I had two great aunts, sisters of my O'Brien grandmother,

Diane Bessel.

who had both married Italians. Great Aunt Beatrice had been the first wife of the famous Guglielmo Marconi (the inventor of radio) and had married Liborio, Marchese Marignoli of Spoleto afterwards. The other aunt, Lilah, was an artist who had married a sculptor.

I had practically no money but luckily at that time the train fare to Rome, in third class, was £9 one way. The train was incredibly uncomfortable with wooden seats all the way. I even had a proposal of marriage from a fat man with baskets of vegetables. We were saved by the wonderful espressos and paninis that were sold up and down the corridors of the train during the journey. At last we arrived.

My first sight of Rome was of a vista of rose coloured buildings in the warm air of the dawn. I will never forget the impression that it made on me. It was quite simply love at first sight: a love that has never left me.

FOUR

La Dolce Vita

W HEN I FIRST ARRIVED IN ROME, money was extremely short. I had a tiny
allowance from my father, which I had to augment. I could not lodge with
my Aunt Bea, as it would have been too expensive, and so she put me in touch
with Donna Maria Marigliano del Monte, a tiny elderly Neapolitan aristocrat
fallen on hard times. She was highly educated and erudite: wonderful company
and full of schemes of all kinds. She would have been called an *imbrogliona*.

She had two rooms to let to recommended visiting foreign girls. When I arrived
there was a tall Scandinavian girl staying, who had a Vespa scooter, which I was
envious of. The rent was ludicrously low, and we did not get much for it.

The house was near the Via Salaria and the Piazza Ungheria, where there was
a famous café where all the foreigners gathered: Polish, Russians, Germans and
other nationalities, mostly on hard times like everyone else. Donna Maria went
there often for tea or espresso to keep up with her friends. Sadly she couldn't
really ask anyone home as there was no money to buy refreshments.

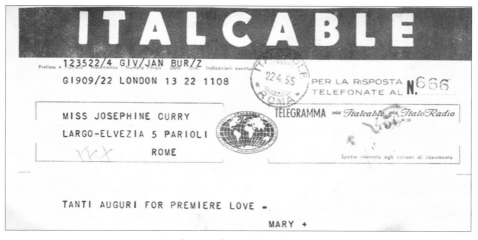

A telegram from Mary Drage.

Dressed for a party in Rome.

She was always immaculately dressed and changed clothes three times a day, as we all did. She always wore a hat and gloves. She went frequently to weddings, funerals, christenings and cocktail parties. She often asked me to accompany her but I hardly ever did as I think she gate-crashed quite a few of them.

Someone had told me that the British Council would be able to find me some work. So I called on them one morning. The director was a hugely fat man and was like a kindly schoolmaster. He found me interpreting jobs. Firstly for the ballet when they came from London, interpreting for the extras for performances and taking them on a tour of Rome. (I had to quickly read up a lot of history.) Then secondly, for a film company which came to Rome and which was led by Sir Michael Balcon. The council also found me jobs with quite a few people who wanted to learn English, including children, who were mostly rather spoilt and badly behaved.

The unreliability of the Italians took a lot of getting used to. Various friends used to talk about plans for the weekend or evenings out: going to the sea for the day or driving to Spoleto. By the time Friday arrived I used to ring them up and talk about the possibilities. Whereupon they often seemed either quite bewildered as to what I was referring to or had simply gone away. I realized that you could never plan anything except at the very last minute when they were on the crest of the wave of an idea which swept them into the plan. It is a completely different mentality. In-between the talk of the first plan they had very likely found something that they preferred to do.

I did suffer a lot of harassment walking along the streets and on public transport, which then only consisted of buses. There were cat calls and whistling and unwelcome passes made on the bus and this all made going out extremely intimidating. I suppose being tall with long blond hair I was a target, especially so soon after the war.

My friend, Cecilia Foley, gave me her dressmaker, Signora Ricci, who lived up four floors in a big building. She was very cheap so I used to spend more money on the material than on having the clothes made.

In the humble trattorias the standard of food was exceptionally high. One could have a three course meal for 500 lira. There were huge helpings. The abbacchio arrosto was a special favourite of mine and there was always a little bag of dried fruit and nuts alongside the plate. Everything was spotless. There was often just a paper tablecloth and sawdust would cover the floor, which was always a hard surface, never carpet. It was a delightful contrast to the grubbiness of England and the smaller restaurants and inedible food. It was all highly seductive.

Rome was enchanting, not least, because of the magnificent surroundings. There was sightseeing on your doorstep, around every corner and in every street. There were great statues and water gushing from the fountains. The towering palazzos and courtyards all had something beautiful to see inside.

Above all I loved the constant warm sunshine and the way it lit up the buildings and seemed to soak into them. You could, by and large, eat out almost every day of the year. The cafés were always packed with people just whiling away the day with an espresso and a newspaper. There was a feeling of complete ease and wellbeing, as if the war had never taken place. Meanwhile the traffic was constantly on the whirl and all the Vespas buzzed in and out of the cars and tore down the little cobbled streets.

I was impressed by the cleanliness of it all. Litter was not thrown about. In the early hours of the morning a big vehicle with brushes and sprinkling water scrubbed all of the streets and pavements.

There were wonderful trips to the opera, memorably to Caracalla where the ancient baths were. We heard *Aida* there and saw real lions, albeit rather drugged. The acoustics were not quite so good as at the Opera House, but it was spectacular to look at: sometimes there was a slight breeze billowing their costumes or a moonlit night, which added to the atmosphere of it all.

I do not think that much has changed in the Eternal City (hence the name). Of course the buildings cannot be tampered with but the people are not as immaculate as they used to be.

* * *

When I went to live in Rome, my great aunt Bea, my paternal grandmother's sister, had already been living there for a number of years. Her name had formerly been O'Brien, as she was one of the fourteen children of Lord Inchiquin. The marriage to Marconi was not a happy one, possibly as he was always working and going abroad. They had lived in Rome and various other places, including on the Isle of Wight, where he did various experiments.

She was handsome and dark haired. She had three children: Giulio, who was rather a fussy semi invalid; Degna, who was beautiful and somewhat formidable; and Gioia who had a pretty sparkling face but was short.

Alas, Marconi had fallen in love with someone else and he and Aunt Bea got divorced. This was shocking in those days. After a while, she married Marchese Liborio Marignoli. He was, according to my father, rather fat and jolly. He did absolutely nothing. He always said, 'moi, je suis un poule de luxe!'

They had one daughter, my beloved Flaminia, and lived in affluence in Rome and at the Villa Redenta outside Spoleto, much of which he owned. The war was terrible for them and their estates were frittered away, sold or confiscated, except for the Villa which they hung on to until Flaminia sold the last bit of land so that we could go on a trip to Milano to visit a man she hoped to marry. Alas, nothing came of it.

During the war Flaminia had married a good-looking American officer and had two boys, Geoffrey and Michael. In the early 1950s, when I was in Rome, they were aged about four and six. It was around this time that Flaminia went to the US with her husband and discovered that his family owned a funeral parlour and a Coca-Cola stand on the road!

So that was the end of him.

Afterwards, back in Rome, Flaminia had a boyfriend called Pier Vittorio, a carabiniere, whom she seemed to like. But they had endless violent rows.

We saw her Torlonia cousins quite a bit. She was very close to them as her father had been Prince Alessandro Torlonia's first cousin.

When I was in Rome, Aunt Bea lived in rather a grand flat in the Via Mangili, amongst the first houses comprising the new district of Parioli, built at the beginning of the twentieth century.

* * *

One day, the British Council contacted me about a possible audition for the part of Kate Pinkerton in *Madame Butterfly,* which a film was being made of (the first I believe). Luckily I got the part, which was exciting and of course lucrative. As most people will know, the part of Kate Pinkerton is very small. Everybody had to be able to read music but almost all of the voices were dubbed – in fact only the tenor, a Greek singer who had sung at La Scala, was recorded.

The work was about ten days of filming. A car filled with chattering Japanese girls turned up for me at Donna Maria's at six o'clock in the morning and we drove to Cinecitta, the film studios. A great deal of time was spent waiting around for hour after hour – then there would be some intense and oft-repeated filming: take after take. The scenery was realistic and the costumes were beautifully made and authentic. My dress was pale mauve taffeta with a large hat.

In all it was a wonderful experience and I was lucky to have come by it.

* * *

Filming for *Madame Butterfly* and a scene from the opera.

Whilst in Rome, I made some new and lasting friendships, not least with the Pecci-Blunts.

Mimi, the matriarch of the family, was a niece of Pope Leo XIII, an eccentric intellectual woman with a forceful personality. She was handsome in a mannish way. She was married to Cecil Blumenthal, who was Jewish and extremely rich. He walked head down and shuffling, with turned in feet. He was kind and straightforward but basically homosexual. His boyfriend, Cecil Everley, was formerly a footman at Madresfield Court (the model for Evelyn Waugh's *Brideshead Revisited*). They were known as 'Les Deux Ceciles'.

Mimi and Cecil had a big family: their children were called Letizia, Viviana, Graziella, Camilla and Dino. They entertained in a lavish style in their huge palazzo, just off the Piazza Venezia. It had its own theatre.

La Marlia, another palace that they had outside Lucca, was formerly the home of Emperor Napoleon's sister, Pauline Borghese. It was a magnificent house, done up in full Empire style, since when it had remained untouched.

Letizia was fanatically socially ambitious and managed to make a good marriage quite early on. When I arrived to live in Rome she was already married to Prince Boncompagni. I went to one memorable party at their palazzo and she wore a beautiful black lace dress over white satin. She was young and handsome. I only got to know Viviana later when she was married and living in South America. Graziella, always my favourite, was married to the Comte Henri de Beaumont, nephew of the Comte Étienne de Beaumont, who had held the famous Paris balls in the 1920s and 30s.

Graziella and Henri had a beautiful apartment in the Palazzo Borghese where the Caccia Club was. It had a lovely old fashioned lift, like a bird cage, with a little velvet sofa to sit on.

Camilla was more bohemian and married an American that she met at the Spoleto festival, who was working with Menotti, called Earl McGrath. He later became a great friend of ours.

Lastly, there was Dino. He was my boyfriend most of the time I was in Rome and therefore, through him, I saw a lot of his family. Dino was wonderfully reliable compared to other admirers that I had. When he used to pick me up

Dino, Letizia and Cecil Pecci-Blunt.

at Donna Maria's he was always exactly forty minutes late, every time, to the minute!

We went to endless parties together: luxurious picnics on beaches, balls, theatres, operas, concerts and amazing dinners at the palazzo Pecci-Blunt, always held in different huge salons or terraces. I have never seen such splendour before, or since, except possibly with the Agnellis in the South of France later on, when I was married.

* * *

Later a girl called Kapi arrived at Donna Maria's. Often we went on trips together to Spoleto.

These Sunday trips included a meeting with an ancient aunt Eloise who had been an opera singer. She looked as if she had come straight from a Victorian portrait. The town was still untouched with little cobbled streets and a beautiful early church with some frescos, which were still visible but faded.

At this time a festival was proposed for August in Spoleto. Filippo Marigholi was very much against the idea and was convinced that it would ruin his beloved town. Actually it did not. Several operas were written and produced by Menotti for the festival, most memorably *The Consul*. There were picture exhibitions and lots of other activities. Celebrities and film stars turned up and it was all most glamorous. The festival went on for many years and probably still does.

The Consul was a terrifying story of a mother and child caught behind the Iron Curtain. The baby was ill and they had trouble with their papers. They had to go every day and queue to see the consul who was behind a glass door and never appeared. The full waiting room was entertained by a macabre conjuror and other strange acts. It all ended in tragedy. It later transferred to a theatre in London and I took my great friend Mary to see it. But she had to leave in the interval, as she got so upset.

FIVE

At Home in Chelsea and Holland Park

AFTER RETURNING FROM ROME, I spent some holidays in Majorca. It was on my return from a trip there that I met Rupert Loewenstein in Oxford, where he had been an undergraduate. In July 1957, we married. He was twenty three and I was twenty six. Everyone said that the age difference was such that it could never last. We were married for fifty seven years.

Rupert had the most wonderful character, which was much shaped by his difficult childhood. He had had a largely absent father who had contributed little to his upbringing, save for the occasional piece of advice on etiquette. His

Rupert as an undergraduate.

Our wedding, 1957, with the parents standing well apart from each other.

mother had treated him, from an early age, as an adult, teaching him how to mix cocktails and encouraging him to become social and gregarious.

Rupert was extremely clever. He won a scholarship to Magdalen College, Oxford, and afterwards he was determined to make money, mostly because of the hopelessness of his family on both sides. His mother and father had had their estates confiscated during and after both world wars and had made do as best as they could in a foreign country, so they had continually been in financial difficulty. This gave Rupert a shaky and alarming view of life on a shoestring. But it certainly fired his ambitions.

Our first house was on St Leonard's Terrace, in Chelsea. It was whilst we were living there that our children were born. I had Rudolf in 1957, prematurely; then Konrad in 1958; and afterwards, Dora, in 1966. By that time we had moved to Holland Park.

When the boys were born I asked my old nanny to come back to us, which I'm glad to say that she did. In a pitch-dark basement our huge dishevelled, Italian cook lived. She always walked around in Rupert's thrown out Dior socks, which had large holes in them. She removed her shoes before answering the door. There was also a daily cleaner.

Rudolf's wax-doll like beauty was much admired when he was a child. He

Rudolf as a small boy.

had very large clear blue eyes and straight flaxen hair with a fringe. His health was delicate but he was unusually clever and had a fanciful turn of mind. He had diligently and determinedly taught himself to read by his third birthday.

* * *

'I can't think of the name of that Mrs. Thingummy's daughter,' said the old nurse.

'Lorraine,' said Rudolf clearly, barely looking up from his game of solitaire.

'That's a good boy,' the nurse responded.

Meanwhile, the younger brother was busy scaling up the bars of the nursery window.

'Come down at once you naughty boy,' called the nurse.

'That boy will be the death of me,' added Rudolf, copying a nanny's old phrase.

His brother's small fists tightened around the bars.

'Nanny told you to come down at once, it's dangerous, did you hear me?' said the nurse.

'That's dangerous,' said the daily.

'Well you won't have that nice orange drink Nanny got you for your tea, we don't like disobedient boys,' she added. His face became purple but he still clung on. She did not like losing face in front of the daily.

'They're usually very good boys' she said.

They went and sat at the table. After a minute or two the brother made a slow dignified descent and went to sit at a small table in the distance, where he quite often sat to establish his independence. He was given his tea, without the orange drink.

The daily was only a fairly efficient cleaner. She resembled a member of a chorus in a bad production of a provincial Italian opera – she was oddly shaped, with a patchy red face in which the crooked features did not fit together at all.

'I'm afraid my Nanny smokes like a chimney,' Rudolf confided to her. (Of course this was not true and was unheard of, in any case.)

* * *

With Konrad after his christening

With Konrad and Rudolf, aged two and three.

Konrad, Rudolf and Eds Somerset at Badminton.

The boys had their coats made at an old fashioned shop called Heyfords at the top of Sloane Street. The assistants were by and large all over sixty years old, but were referred to as 'the young ladies.' I was very particular about colour and bought moss green material for one winter. This was not among the patterns at the shop. They only had blue, red and possibly fawn. The old nurse said she was ashamed to be seen with Rudolf and his brother in the park with these coats.

On Thursdays the nurses had their day off.

'What a beautiful colour that is,' said one young mother as she pushed her pram past us.

'Wherever did you find that divine material?' asked another.

The boys smiled sweetly and trailed their pure white gloves along the wall as I pushed them home. They were put to bed at least half an hour earlier than usual. Instead of carrying them down a steep flight of stairs to the bathroom I put them into the nursery sink. They quite enjoyed this, as a good deal of water got spilt.

* * *

About once a month the boys' paternal grandfather came to tea. He was tall and formidable and not used to children. They did not like him. 'You should be kind to Grandpa, and even if you don't like him, you must pretend to,' said the nurse.

They made a great effort, and were as charming and enchanting as only they knew how. As a result of this, their grandfather was seen to warm, and respond, and even smile. When six o'clock came he rose to go.

'Say goodbye nicely to Grandpa,' said the nurse.

'Goodbye, goodbye!' they piped.

Rudolf led him to the door.

'You know we were only pretending to like you Grandpa,' he said pleasantly.

* * *

Later they went to a small school nearby, where they wore blue uniforms. They made some friends and often there was talk of future careers. Rudolf had a friend at this time, that he often talked about.

'So what is your friend going to do when he grows up?' I asked.

Rudolf replied that he was going to become a priest and go on to be Pope.

* * *

Once, after we had gone to India, the boys' nurse took them to lunch at their maternal grandfather's house. He was away at the time. Miss Dorrit, his housekeeper, had made them toad-in-the-hole. She was small and round and brightly coloured. She always wore a wig and a hat. The nurse did not approve of her as she smoked and wore make up. But it was said that she had also once been a nanny.

'What lovely boys they are,' she said. 'You just sit down and I'll get you a tasty lunch.'

The table reached practically up to their chins. They ate slowly and thoughtfully as the two adults rattled on headlong with their chat. The boys finished every scrap on their plates.

'Well,' Rudolf smilingly remarked, as he placed his knife and fork neatly together, 'that was really nasty'.

The nurse and Miss Dorrit were far too busy gossiping to hear.

* * *

Dora's first Holy Communion.

A few years later, Dora was born. The boys were concerned, as she did not arrive complete with long curly hair.

At the christening an elegant French lady godmother asked Rudolf if he loved his sister.

'No,' he replied 'but I am glad that she has God in her now.'

Rudolf later became a mathematics teacher and is now a Friar of the Dominican Order. He is still teaching.

* * *

Much has been written about old English nannies over the years. I had experience of them before the Second World War as a child and afterwards when they were fading out, in favour of aux pairs. My son Konrad always thought that this was spelt 'old pears'.

The original old-fashioned nanny usually started as a junior nursery maid; if it was a large family there could have been possibly two or even three nursery maids. Then, if suitable, she was promoted when the nanny retired or died.

I thought of nannies as armoured warriors: dressed always in grey in a phalanx protecting the children from the world at large and possibly from their parents, or near relations, who had no experience of looking after children and probably did not want to. Such was the social calendar . . . Weekend parties, shoots, tennis parties, dinners, teas, lunch parties. Ascot, the Derby, Cowes, shooting in Scotland, and trips abroad sailing on yachts. It was non stop. Parents did not have the time to look after their children and above all, it was not the fashion to do so.

The children were dressed up and brought down to see their parents between 5.30 and 6 p.m. – not long enough to become a nuisance. And then they were swept away to bed.

On occasions when the parents were going out to dinner they would sometimes come up and kiss the children goodnight in their beds, if time allowed. They were always dressed in their finery.

If the parents had country estates the children would go for holidays there but always with the same nannies accompanying them.

When I was a child, sometimes parents were so busy that they sent their

A group of nannies keep watch over their charges at a family birthday party at St Leonard's Terrace.

Nanny Proctor and Nanny Phillips, mine and Sebastian Yorke's nannies at Ledbury.

children to Nanny's home when she took her holiday. Some holiday! That actually never happened to me but a temporary nanny was hired instead for the two weeks that she was away. Also, when I was young, my mother hired a temporary nanny even on the nanny's day off (usually a Thursday). All of the nannies had the same day off, so that they could meet up and gossip.

In the morning the nannies wore a grey skirt, a blouse and an apron. In the afternoon, they changed into a grey suit, skirt and jacket or coat, a crêpe de Chine blouse, sensible brown or black walking shoes, a grey felt hat and gloves.

The children were immaculately dressed in dresses or little suits with tweed coats over the top when chilly, plus hat and white gloves. A tricycle or scooter was allowed if the park was not too far away. When my boys were in a pram the nanny would wheel them from St Leonard's Terrace to Hyde Park where they met all the other nannies in the Daisy Walk. Most of the families knew each other well, so there was plenty to talk about.

There could be jealousy between the nannies. On one occasion when my boys were about four and five my mother's great friend who was in waiting to the Queen was asked by Her Majesty to find some children to keep Prince Andrew company while watching the Changing of the Guard. The nanny of the children who were usually invited for this, spotted our children, from below, at a window of Buckingham Palace with *their* nanny. Next day in the park she said to my nanny, somewhat indignantly, 'What on earth were you and your boys doing in Buckingham Palace, nanny?'

They always called each other nanny.

When I first married I was intent on looking after the boys myself. Of course it was impossible; again due to all the business activities and social life that we led at the time. It was even then a struggle to insist that I had them on nanny's day off and during her holiday. But I stuck religiously to this rule. My own nanny had retired but she willingly came to help out when Rudolf was born and was wonderfully helpful, reliable and kind – though rather domineering of course.

Cooking was something the nannies never did. They did the washing, ironing, sewing, in fact everything pertaining to the children: except cooking. They were often excellent seamstresses and made beautiful muslin dresses and smocking and all manner of delicate garments.

When the boys were two and three we took them to Rome, where Rupert was working at the time. We took a flat at the top of a hotel on the Via Boncompagni, off the Via Veneto. It was spacious and old-fashioned and had a view of the Borghese gardens. My nanny was overwhelmed by Rome: particularly by the wonderful weather and everyone sitting out in the cafes late at night. I don't think she had ever been abroad before.

'What do you think of it all?' I said to her.

'Well, it could be anywhere,' she replied.

I asked Nancy Mitford what she thought nanny had meant and she replied, 'Paradise of course!'

We had a wonderful time and I loved it as I always hated leaving the boys behind when we went on trips.

We went to the beach at Ostia early every day and lo and behold we found some English grey nannies. One of whom was Nanny Borghese who had been with the family for something like forty years. The nannies were always called by the family they worked for.

On her day off, our nanny went on a tour of Rome on a bus. She just couldn't believe her eyes and she did not even grumble about the heat.

* * *

We moved to Holland Villas Road in 1964 as St Leonard's Terrace had become too small and somehow Rupert's business was looking up a bit.

It was then quite a shabby road of lovely big early nineteenth century houses, with spacious rooms. We had half an acre of garden. It was an impossible dream.

As at St Leonard's I wanted John Fowler to help me with décor as much as we could afford. We had big green patterned wallpaper on white in the dining room and a pretty carved wooden mantelpiece, which was a lot less expensive than marble.

In the drawing room I decided on yellow walls. Fowler chose material for the sofas and chairs that I didn't really like too much. He was so formidable and had a temper always just on the edge of exploding, so I didn't say anything. I suppose that this was rather weak of me.

The first floor and nursery floor I decorated myself and really enjoyed creating.

We had a blue, white and gold library where we had the television. It was a double fronted house so there were four rooms on each floor. It was a wonderful place to live: the garden was all lawn surrounded by mature trees, a huge plane tree and a beautiful mulberry at the end, planted as part of the avenue from Kensington Palace by King Charles II. Along the left side was a brick path which I laid myself, while expecting my daughter, with a flower bed along its length against the wall.

We had several friends also living in the road, which was great fun. I bought the bricks for the path from my friend Lindy Dufferin who lived on our side, and still does, in a much bigger house, but with a smaller garden.

The road and Holland Park in general went up enormously in value over the years and became very fashionable.

We did a great deal of entertaining: both business and social. I did enjoy it but it made me somewhat nervous, as the domestic help was far from expert. We certainly had some scoundrels. It was sad that Carisma (our Italian cook at St Leonard's Terrace) didn't feel she was up to staying with us, as she wanted to retire. Also, my own nanny, who had been with me all through the boys' upbringing, had to retire.

The lack of good domestic help clouded everything. We had a series of Italian couples, including one called Luigi and Pierina, of whom we were fond. But then we discovered that Luigi beat Pierina up, when she would appear with bruises on her face. I got involved in their quarrels, which was stupid of me. I tried to keep them apart but it didn't work. They all had to go in the end.

My father took over the basement and made a beautiful flat and big drawing room on the garden where he had his grand piano. His housekeeper used to babysit when we went out.

* * *

Konrad and Rudolf with Dora and her dog Hector at our farmhouse outside Hungerford.

One Christmas, we had a difficult assortment of in-laws coming: nobody really got on with anyone else. And that was putting it mildly. The whole thing became a problem and we debated whether to have them all together and risk open warfare, or whether to invite them in separate pairs. They were all married again except my mother, so it was seven in all.

This particular Christmas, we had Rupert's mother and stepfather and my mother.

Our country house was a 1660 manor house, which I had come to dislike. The two mothers were totally unacceptable to each other. Rupert's mother was a hard drinker, a talented sculptress and artistic in a Parisian-café sort of way. She was generous, warm-hearted and thoroughly bohemian. The stepfather was a genial weak Jewish American who looked like the majority of Hollywood producers. Only he wasn't one.

Rudolf, my eldest son, dreaded the grandmothers meeting more than anyone, as he was devoted to both of them. He spent most of Christmas playing an old gramophone in his attic sitting-room. He deigned to appear at present giving, where he spent most of the time consigning the torn Christmas paper to the fire.

On the first evening the grandmothers were careful, though my mother saw fit to cut up her spaghetti with a knife and fork in order to annoy Rupert's mother, who was a passionate Italophile.

At Christmas lunch stories of various burglaries were discussed. Once, Rupert's mother told us, she had run out of her house after a thief and caught him, brought him back, given him several glasses of wine and relieved him of the silver. He became quite a friend in the end. It was a magnificent story.

My mother said, 'I just don't believe it, you couldn't possibly have done that, you've made it all up.'

It was in fact true which made it all the more bitter. Rupert's mother burst into tears. Rudolf rapidly left the table.

My mother, triumphant, started on one of her burglar stories which was equally amazing, and terrifying, but everyone's tempers were frayed by then and furthermore they knew the story already.

Rupert's mother, fortified by a large brandy, went into the kitchen and fished the empty caviar tin out of the rubbish bin to see if there was any left. The two younger children followed her out and were convulsed with mirth. She cut her finger badly as a result, and had to be led away to bed.

By now I was livid and exhausted. Going into the study I found the stepfather already dipping into an expensive box of chocolates intended as a present for someone else. My own mother had become very sweet as if butter wouldn't have melted in her mouth. She was sitting there quietly reading some delightful story to Dora as if nothing had happened.

A few days later we gave another dinner in London for Rupert's father and step-mother. My aunt Dig and my mother were also invited.

We had an Irish manservant at that time, who came once a week to do odd jobs. His name was Mr Rush. I thought that he was the closest thing to a leprechaun that one would ever encounter. He was small, delicate and pale with a long sharp nose like Pinocchio. His black hair stood up in a shock on his head; he was always neatly dressed and carried a carefully furled umbrella. The housekeeper at the time, Mrs Dunlop, couldn't abide him, so when he came round he was not allowed in the kitchen and had to clean the silver on Dora's nursery floor and eat his packed lunch there too. He used to disturb her while she tried to do her homework at a little desk in her bedroom by hopping in on her pogo stick, trying to persuade her to chat. She was very conscientious over her schoolwork and always sent him packing.

He was asked to help at Christmas dinner. As luck would have it his brother arrived back from Australia that very afternoon without prior notice. He had not seen him for ten years. Mr Rush was a very kind family-minded man and the emotional intensity of the reunion all proved a bit too much for him and he had several drinks to fortify himself. Unlike most Irishmen, he did not ever normally drink.

Towards the evening he rang me with a slurred voice. He asked me whether he could bring his sister Winnie and her husband Rawlston to help out. I agreed that he could.

They all arrived very late. The guests were already assembled, quietly drinking champagne in the drawing room. I was trying to lay the table, thinking that Rush and his entourage were not coming.

'I told you that man Rush was no good,' said Mrs Dunlop disagreeably.

Rawlston turned out to be a Pakistani and his wife Winnie was a typical cosy-looking, fat Irish woman with a comforting manner.

We went through to the dining room and by this point Mr Rush was dangerously drunk. We all finally sat down at the table. Rupert rose and went to carve the turkey but Rush had already lifted it up on its huge platter, which he could barely carry, and started to hand it around. He was quickly relieved of it and led away into the kitchen to sit down. We continued without him.

To make up for this, after dinner he came and asked if he could sing 'Silent Night' to the guests, accompanied on the piano by Winnie. I groaned inwardly but said that he could. He sang very well and elegantly in Gaelic. The guests had not really noticed that anything was wrong at all. They swept away in their various mini cabs exclaiming about what a lovely evening it had been.

SIX

Life in the Fast Lane

WHEN WE LIVED ON HOLLAND VILLAS ROAD, my husband's work as a stockbroker meant that we started to enjoy a much more high powered social life. Rupert bought a bank called Leopold Joseph with Alexis de Redé, Sir Anthony Berry (who later died in the Brighton bombing) and Jonathan Guinness, now Lord Moyne. This was all successful and led to Rupert being introduced, by our friend Christopher Gibbs, to the Rolling Stones in about 1970. Afterwards Rupert took on their finances.

Much of social life in those days was dominated by what was called café society. What a strange phenomenon café society is! Has it always existed? Supposedly, it is all about the high fashion of the time and constructed along hard and fast rules for clothes, behaviour, and manners. Indeed, café society is a construction to which you must rigidly conform if you wish to remain invited and acceptable – otherwise you are cast out.

When I lived in Rome at the end of the war, society was divided into the so-called Black and White families. The Black families, being of ancient lineage, still lived in various states of decay or splendour in their palazzos. They wore dowdy clothes and were aristocratic, deeply religious and had perfect manners. They often included plain, worn-looking spinster sisters and daughters and studious sons wearing spectacles. They were generally responsible and conscientious.

The White families were different. To be acceptable, you had to be either beautiful, famous, rich, the possessor of great wit or well born. This society mixed with celebrities such as film and opera stars. They had yachts, beautiful cars and haute couture clothes. If you were a part of this group, then you could only be seen at certain restaurants or nightclubs that were in fashion at the time. Adulterous affairs, of which there were many, were conducted with the utmost discretion and secrecy. Appearances meant everything.

I remember one glamorous couple in particular. Having been highlights of this group they lost a large amount of money and had to downsize their house and

Gianni Agnelli and me at our first big party at St Moritz.

car. They were not invited much anymore and were treated with quiet disdain.

Once accepted into the group you were automatically invited to all the parties, expeditions and picnics. This whole way of life was the same in Paris and New York and everyone knew each other. Conversation was generally superficial, sometimes cruel and essentially gossipy. We gave our first 'society' party in St Moritz in the late 1950s. It was there that we met the Agnellis for the first time.

Alexis de Redé's dinners, parties and balls were certainly magnificent – and held in splendid settings. Most of the organisation was concentrated on the food, drinks, table, settings and flowers. But not much focus was placed on ensuring that the guests were in any way interesting or had good conversation. I always felt I had on a straightjacket of boredom when I was at one of these parties. I would feel completely trapped. I do not speak French well and that may have been part of the reason why. That is entirely my fault. I learnt Italian in the old days in Rome, but never liked the French language.

In New York Mrs Gilbert Miller was one of the leaders of café society. This was in the 1960s, 70s and 80s. A friend of hers, a chic little lady, once waltzed in late for a lunch party that Kitty Miller was giving. She said to the guests that had gathered, 'I'm so sorry I am late but I had to pop into Cartier to buy my maid a present.' (It was Christmas at the time).

Kitty replied in her slow American drawl, 'Well if you only have one maid, then you can afford to go to Cartier!'

Dancing with Erwein Gaetchman.

* * *

Kitty Miller, née Bache, was in her seventies when I first knew her. Money was no object for her and so she was advised by the leading decorators and florists of the day.

She had a house on South Street in Mayfair, run with a full staff. She also had a home in New York and a luxurious villa on Majorca, in the days when it was unspoilt.

She was unusually ugly and had a heavy build and a long face. She was slightly hunch-backed. She did not have much hair – and that which she did have was

With Tom Parr on Kitty Miller's motor yacht.

dyed a blue mauve.

Her exquisite couture clothes were immaculate; she wore unsurpassed jewellery and accessories, all of which were a joy to look at. She had a sharp wit which often took one by surprise.

Kitty was very hospitable but only to the fashionable folk of the moment. She gave cocktail parties, dinners, bridge dinners and balls throughout the year.

Her annual ball was held in the River Room at the Savoy. Various couples gave dinner parties beforehand and then everyone went on to the ball at 10 p.m. This was all followed by a lavish breakfast after midnight.

She once very kindly lent us her villa in Majorca when I was expecting my daughter. That was in April.

It rained everyday.

* * *

With Alexis de Redé and Dino Pecci-Blunt.

Alexis de Redé was, for a long time, a leader of café society. He was, I think, a very strange person. He was handsome in an effete and fair way, with a perfect figure: and always beautifully and appropriately dressed with shining handmade shoes.

But basically he did not speak – I do not know why, it was probably because of a deep shyness – so when he did, everyone waited with bated breath to hear his few quiet words or pronouncements. It was said that he was silent in four languages!

He was very generous and clever and was a great help to my husband in the early days of his career, when they owned a bank together.

I think his main attribute was his exquisite taste. He was close to the Paris Rothschilds, Guy and Marie-Hélène, and had magnificent Versailles-like apartments in the Hotel Lambert, formerly owned by the Czartoriskis, and later the Counts Zamoyski. He entertained lavishly for many years. His close companion and protector was the Chilean multi-millionaire, Arturo Lopez, also famous for his parties and sharp wit. They were the ultimate high fashion icons. They entertained politicians, artists, film stars, aristocrats and royalty. Alexis had many wonderful works of art and the best French furniture. His apartment on the piano nobile had high ceilings and wonderful parquet floors and an ancient long gallery where he often gave large parties. The rooms had tall

The invitation to the Oriental Ball and Rupert and me at the Ball.

windows looking over the Seine.

We went on many trips with him. He always brought his own bedding: linen sheets, pillows and lots of cashmere rugs and blankets. Arturo Lopez had given a great deal of money for the restoration of Versailles and we went there many times. We also went to St Moritz, where he had a permanent apartment in the Palace Hotel. Alexis was invaluable in assisting at the great balls given by the Rothschilds at Ferrières, their country mansion, near Paris.

The Proust Ball was the most spectacular with 1,500 guests. The costumes were the most authentic and beautifully made and, because of the theme, they corresponded perfectly with the house and its elaborate, rich, turn-of-the-century décor. They covered the whole house – which was enormous – with cobwebs, and lit it up to look like moonlight. It had to be seen to be believed.

Alexis always had dachshunds. They were invariably disagreeable, probably because they were often left with servants who did not care for them. They had elegant collars, harnesses and leads with gold trimmings.

Alexis seemed to live a very eighteenth century kind of life of exquisite lunches on uncomfortable little gold chairs with breathtakingly rich food served on beautifully decorated tables and silver bowls of roses sprayed lightly with water to look like dew. Though there were always interesting and famous people there, I always felt terribly bored and claustrophobic and couldn't wait to get away.

Over the years I saw many photographs of Alexis with various celebrities, including the Duchess of Windsor, Maria Callas and the President of France. He seemed to me like a wood or cardboard cut-out, lifelessly placed in a group, or propped up next to a celebrity.

He grew weak towards the end of his life but had a charming lady companion, Charlotte Aillaud, a sister of Juliette Gréco, with whom he also travelled.

He died in 2004.

* * *

The Agnellis were at the highest peak of café society from the 1950s onwards. Marella Agnelli was born a Princess Caracciolo, from the South of Italy, in Naples. She was exceptionally tall and as elegant as a swan, with the most beautiful neck and aquiline nose. She married Gianni Agnelli in 1953. He was one of the most attractive men most people had ever seen – dashing with slanting eyes and black wavy hair. He was a tireless womaniser.

When I lived in Rome I never met the Agnellis, though I mixed with many of their friends. After I married we met in St Moritz. I arrived alone at the Palace

With Gioconda Cicogna at La Leopolda.

Hotel early one winter, as Rupert could not come over for a few days.

Sam Spiegel, the film producer, invited me to have drinks in the bar where there were several friends of his including Marella. She seemed to take to me and asked for my number, and from then on we became friends. The house parties they held in the South of France were legendary. Their villa, La Leopolda, was formerly the home of Leopold I, King of the Belgians. It was a magnificent house perched high up above St Jean and with a splendid view. Usually there were about twenty guests staying, of all nationalities. There was a fleet of beautiful little white Fiat cars (Gianni was President of Fiat) with straw roofs like golf buggies. You could take one and drive yourself off anywhere you liked. I was quite stunned by the luxury. I'd never before dreamed of such glamour.

Of course I worried about clothes, but I managed somehow. Virginia, my Cypriot dressmaker, rose to the occasion and was worked off her feet. *L'Officiel*, the haute couture magazine, had the most wonderful photographs of the latest fashions from Paris and Italy. We spent a lot of time copying various dresses.

When we had lunch or dinner at La Leopolda we always had it in a different great salon each time. Inside or outside, there were fleets of servants everywhere. We usually spent the day on one of the various yachts or speed boats that the Agnellis had, and often had lunch on one of the small islands off the coast. Gianni always liked to go out when there was a storm, and when all the red warning flags were up I used to go along, but it was at times really hair-raising.

His driving was reckless. Once, returning to the villa from Cannes I asked him to stop at a hotel on the road as I was too terrified to continue. I ordered a cab to take me home. He was most contemptuous but I think that it was the right decision, as he completely bashed up his leg after crashing in one of the tunnels on the Riviera. He never walked normally again.

We all used to go to the casino in Monte Carlo quite often. Gianni would gamble recklessly and then disappear on his yacht for a day or two with the favourite girl of the moment. He was easily bored and never did the same thing for long – except his work, which he took seriously.

The Agnellis also had a private plane, like the other rich people of their ilk, such as Stavros Niarchos and Heini Thyssen. Occasionally we were lent a plane to fly back to London.

I will never forget the beauty of the garden, flowers and décor and the glamour of the guests. There was such a carefree atmosphere of pure pleasure at La Leopolda, where there was also a circular swimming pool.

The Agnellis did however have a lot of tragedies in their life later on: including illness and the suicide of their son.

* * *

We first met the Duke and Duchess of Windsor at a dinner party given at Maxim's in Paris.

I remember sitting on the Duke's right. As I was married to a German he presumed that I spoke the language. He was rather disappointed when I said that I didn't, and told me that he always loved to speak it whenever possible. I told him that my uncle Arthur Paget had been an equerry to Queen Mary.

'You mean my mother?' he asked.

Normally in England one would have received a rebuke if one had talked of 'your mother' to any member of the Royal Family – but by this time he had become estranged from the world of Royal etiquette.

The Duke was much smaller than I expected him to be and neat and shriveled looking. The Duchess was like a lively, smart marmoset, and the most brilliant mimic. At one point during the dinner the Duke asked the musicians who were playing at each table in turn, to play him a favourite tune. The Duchess got up and scampered round the table and blew him up and said, 'I told you never to ask for that song again.' She was surprisingly agitated and he looked most dejected afterwards, poor thing.

At the other end of the table sat Prince Johannes Thurn und Taxis, an old friend of ours and a fiendish character. He had said to me before dinner that it was enough to make loud sounds imitating the German language for the Duke to get thoroughly excited, replying 'Ja Ja sehr gut' and so on. This was put into action and worked just as planned. But though we did get a bit hysterical, no one seemed to be any the wiser.

We met the Windsors again many times but I do not remember a single interesting thing that they either did or said.

* * *

In the 1970s we were invited to Royal Lodge, Windsor for the weekend. This was a great excitement as it was where the Queen Mother and Princess Margaret spent most weekends.

We arrived at about 6.30pm and were shown into a large drawing room overlooking a wide terrace. Over the mantlepiece was the famous portrait of George IV with a curl of hair over his forehead. Some of the other guests had arrived already, most of whom we knew. Our hostesses were extremely welcoming and after a drink Queen Elizabeth said to me, 'Perhaps you would like me to take you up to your room?'

The house had at least three floors. We went on, led by her, up and up, whilst she talked non-stop.

'I always think this house is a bit like a hotel,' she said, laughing gaily.

After a bit she stopped and asked whether I could pick up a hairpin that had fallen out of her hair.

'They are impossible to buy these days you know,' she said.

I picked them up at intervals as they fell out. They were perfectly ordinary little hairpins available in every chemist!

We got to our floor, which was really quite chilly.

Queen Elizabeth said, 'Oh dear, I hope you'll be warm enough.'

I assured her that I would be.

The bathroom had a linoleum floor and was extremely old fashioned and rather like those we had at boarding school.

We got ready for dinner and all assembled in the drawing room again. I came down a little early and found the Queen Mother in a corner of the drawing room by the gramophone, dancing.

'How I love this song. It's called "Manhattan Madness",' she said to me.

She had such a merry love of life, which was completely captivating. At dinner we were too many ladies and so I sat on her right. I reminded her that she had had drawing lessons with my mother and aunt at their house in Lowndes Street in the twenties. She did not remember this and looked rather blank.

On Saturday she took me to see the little house that the Welsh people had made for the Princesses when they were children. She walked ahead of me down a narrow path with her corgi trotting behind her. Every now and then it turned round and snarled at me. I was swinging my shoulder bag to and fro while I walked and it happened to hit the little dog on the nose. After that it calmed down. The house was very pretty. The front door was about four feet high. It was the most perfect thing for children.

Later there was talk of plans to go to church the following morning.

'Well you know where to go don't you,' Princess Margaret said. (This was because our sons were at a nearby prep school called Scaitcliffe and they went to a little local Catholic church nearby. The church was a sort of Nissen hut).

'Oh no, of course they don't want to go there. They will want to come with us and see what's going on,' said the Queen Mother. Poor Princess Margaret was duly squashed.

On Sunday morning we walked to the small chapel in the grounds. As we arrived two large cars drew up and the Queen and Prince Philip and some other members of the Royal Family alighted. We were directed into a small room to the right of the altar. Part of the column had been removed by Queen Victoria so that she could observe the congregation. There was strict placement. We sat either side of the Queen. I think she probably thought that we were visiting Germans as all the way through the service she found the places in her prayer book and kindly pointed them out for me. They all came back to Royal Lodge for drinks but did not stay for lunch.

We left in the afternoon and went back to our little farmhouse near Hungerford. Some time later we were invited again but sadly we were unable to go.

* * *

We really met and got to know Princess Margaret on Mustique. She and Rupert got on well immediately. I once asked Mick Jagger why he thought that this was so.

'Cos they're a couple of Huns!' he replied.

Our favourite photograph of Princess Margaret, taken by Reinaldo Herrera.

But I think really it was because they were both well informed about history and religion and because of their shared German blood.

At first I found Princess Margaret rather intimidating, but as we got to know one another better we grew much closer. She was an extraordinarily good and loyal friend and always sympathetic and caring if you were ill. She was most hospitable and had perfect manners.

She loved to have a singsong at the piano and could sing most hymns by heart. Like the Queen Mother she adored a party and Colin Tennant would always organize one for her at the drop of a hat – especially on Mustique.

Once, on Mustique, Princess Margaret came over to our house to swim in our pool and have lunch with us. On arrival, she expressed a wish to go to the bathroom.

'Oh, mine is an awful mess as the maid is hopeless,' I said, shuddering at the thought of her seeing it.

I suggested that she might use a different one in the house.

'No, I will go to your bathroom,' she responded.

She was in there a long time and I began to get worried that perhaps she wasn't well. But then the door suddenly opened and she appeared triumphantly.

'Well,' she said, 'I have cleaned the whole bathroom up for you.'

I was quite touched and surprised by this.

* * *

Every Christmas Princess Margaret used to go to Asprey with several men friends, including Rupert, to buy a present for us and vice versa.

Ladies were not allowed! They had a good lunch beforehand and then went on a great shop.

Princess Margaret loved looking at all the luxury goods and took her time, perusing various things that she fancied. She always made clear what she would like and luckily was mindful of the cost. Rupert then bought her the present. Once

Rupert on a business call.

she couldn't find anything that she wanted to give us and said in her high pitched, slow voice, 'Well there's nothing here, but I have something at home that you'd really love,' – so they went off to Kensington Palace where she produced a pink cachepot, which she duly presented to him. It has been useful but isn't at all pretty.

Colin Glenconner once gave her a really beautiful gold box for an important birthday. I think that it was for her fiftieth. I saw it and said, 'what a beautiful box!'

'No, I don't like it at all,' she replied. 'I would much rather have a really useful present like a hot water bottle cover.'

My mother was always brilliant about presents. In the days when I had my fractures and was particularly worn out at Christmas time she would say, 'I know what I want for a present' and would tell me what it was.

'I will get it and wrap it up and give it to you and you can give it to me on Christmas Day.'

So we did this and she pretended it was a surprise and said, 'Thank you so much darling, it's just what I wanted.' She was very kind about those sorts of things.

I find coffee table books a menace. They are easy to give but invariably weigh a ton. Sometimes they are even too heavy to put on your lap. Of such books Diana Cooper used to say: 'It's not a question of not being able to put it down, but not being able to pick it up in the first place!' Normal books, especially history books, are also often colossal. My friend Anne Somerset wrote a brilliant biography of Elizabeth I. It was huge. I was deep into it and going away for a few days so I cut it in half but sadly all the pages flew out and floated about. So that was no good.

It would be a good idea to have several volumes in a box instead. But I suppose that this would be too expensive?

* * *

When my husband started to manage the financial affairs of the Rolling Stones we became great friends with the band and travelled with them on many of their tours.

I remember one concert, in Paris, particularly well.

The scene, as you stepped out of the revolving doors into the lobby of the hotel where the band were staying, resembled a gipsy encampment. The harassed concierge and his underlings were desperately trying to answer hundreds of unfamiliar questions. Photographers were inside and out. All the little tables were crowded with trendy looking children of all ages and their even trendier young nannies. Bemused waiters scurried about, not to speak of room service, which was stretched to the limit. Every few yards, there stood a huge bodyguard, some of them black, with flexing muscles and earphones. Personal assistants hurried about

with clipboards, always searching for someone. There were friends who followed the show, some trusted fans and a posse of spectacular models in micro skirts strolling languidly about.

Every few hours one of the stars would appear or step out of the lift. At this point there would be a slight hush over the crowd and also a general movement, as people hoped to be noticed. Occasionally Mick Jagger would walk through the lobby but he usually took a service lift and left by a back door to avoid the crowds outside.

Mick Jagger was of medium height and sallow with shoulder length brown hair. He had unusually high cheekbones and thick lips. His figure was as trim as could be with tiny hips and thin legs.

At about five o'clock he appeared. He wore a brilliant pea green Harris Tweed suit of conventional cut over a white T-shirt and spotless gym shoes with small holes cut out all over them.

He looked warily about from under his brows at the models, without meeting anybody's eye – an enormously broad, squat black bodyguard, who had the sweetest smile imaginable, accompanied him.

Several people attempted to waylay the star, but he went briskly on with his loping walk, out through the revolving doors. The police quickly carved a path for him through the avidly waiting crowd. He ran and jumped into a stretch limo and was borne away.

Mick Jagger and Rupert discussing business on Mustique.

There was plenty to look at in the lobby that day. The lead guitarist suddenly lurched out of the lift in a long black coat, clutching a bottle of vodka in one hand. Keith Richards was of sinister aspect: he had cultivated this image over many years and now it had become a part of him. His hair was black and untidily spiked. It stood out around his head, and his ear sported a skull and cross bones earring.

His beautiful wife and two small ash blond daughters accompanied him. Belying his appearance he was nearly always in a jovial mood and behaved affectionately to all and sundry. His wife was warm and kind with wonderful manners and so were his daughters.

Mick later returned and was to be seen in deep consultation with his personal assistant and one of the models. A few hours before the show he conferred with Rupert about his choice of neckwear for an after the show party that night. The choice was between a diamond choker and a large bow tie measuring about twelve inches in breadth. The bow tie won the day.

A few hours before the show went on at the biggest stadium in Paris, holding

75,000 spectators, buses collected outside the hotel. The crowd was moved away. Members of the tour were issued with a confusing array of different badges. These gave them access to backstage, on stage, the mixer plus the various VIP lounges, where a great deal of food and drink was available.

The friends and fans that were lucky enough to have a VIP badge always thought that they were in the right lounge, but unbeknown to them, there were three. In the highest-grade room were the children of the stars, mostly seated in front of a giant television portraying the concert, as it was too dangerous and noisy to go out and watch it from the audience. The personal assistants were to be found there and the wives of the various managers.

Occasionally the Stones themselves wandered in from their dressing rooms or caravans. Special food was made for them at their request, but they did not often eat it. On one fateful occasion, Keith decided he would like some shepherd's pie, which was always there for him. That night, as luck would have it, some guests had eaten it and nothing was left. It was about twenty minutes before the curtain was due to rise.

Firstly there was a burst of furious swearing, at which people stood rooted to the spot. Then, the guitarist drew an ugly long knife out of his belt and demanded another shepherd's pie be brought up, otherwise he would not go on stage. It was an alarming scene, as the guests backed away, fearful of the violence of his temper. The show would have to be delayed even longer. It was already over the forty five minutes of mandatory waiting time, imposed in order to rev the audience up to the point of hysteria.

Like a miracle, but mostly due to the modern invention of the microwave, a pie was found, which he duly ate. The star grinned from ear to ear as if to say, 'Gotcha!'

And then they were off.

The audience was a sea of waving arms and roared like a vast ocean in a storm. Everything and everybody was borne along as if on a fast moving tide. The deafening music, wild beat and myriad of coloured lights and beams swept you along for two hours and then it was all over.

Before the final item, there was a spectacular firework display. The Stones were quickly spirited with their aides into waiting limos backstage and were probably back at the hotel before the audience had finished applauding.

* * *

Rupert was unable to go to the wedding of Mick and Bianca Jagger, which was at St Tropez. He asked me to go to represent him. I was not well at the time and it was the last thing that I wanted to do. I decided however that I had better go. We all stayed at the Hotel outside St Tropez. I think it all lasted for about three days. Ahmet Ertegun, head of Atlantic Records and a close friend of ours was there, so I had some support.

On the first morning I came down and had breakfast with Keith Richards, who was sitting alone in the courtyard. He was so bright and amusing and we had a really good chat. The civil wedding was at the town hall in a little square. We all gathered outside. Ahmet hired a sports car and we whirled about in that. Keith was late for the ceremony and I remember seeing him banging on the door to be let in.

There was then a white wedding in a church nearby. Bianca looked quite beautiful in a St Laurent white suit and large shady hat. The press were everywhere and Patrick Lichfield was taking photographs. I wore a mauve jacket with leg of mutton sleeves and a three-quarter length skirt, along with a mauve boater with red cherries on it. In the sixties you could wear anything and the more like fancy dress it was, the better.

There was a huge evening party which took place in a theatre. Many celebrities came, including all the Beatles. A lot of people performed on stage and Mick sang with a famous jazz singer.

There were a good deal of substances going around.

* * *

One day my husband told me that the Stones wanted to donate a certain amount of money to charity. They had asked him for some advice, so he asked me for my thoughts. I immediately suggested the Menuhin School for music in Surrey, which was in those days in its infancy and had been founded by Yehudi Menuhin, the famous violinist. The Stones agreed.

One of my first great musical experiences was hearing Yehudi Menuhin play at the Albert Hall. It must have been about 1948. (My mother was very good about the arts and always took me to concerts and picture exhibitions.) On the occasion that I saw Menuhin for the first time, he played the Beethoven violin concerto. I was completely swept away and felt transported for a short time into paradise. It was at that moment that I understood what Einstein had meant, when he said, after listening to Yehudi play, 'Now I know there is a God in heaven.'

At the time that the Stones decided to donate some money, their opening night was looming at the Earls Court Stadium and Yehudi sent a message that he would be interested to hear them. I thought immediately that this would be a great mistake. Menuhin's highly tuned ears and sensitivity would never be able to bear the deafening cacophony of a rock concert. After a week or so he contacted us again and insisted on coming. We invited him to dinner before and then to go on to the concert with us. As it happened the opening was important and featured a lotus flower, which slowly opened to reveal the band. I particularly wanted him to see this.

We waited and waited for Yehudi to arrive at our house in Holland Park. At last he appeared clutching a bunch of gladioli. The dietary requests had been complicated, but in view of the time he hardly touched a morsel and we had to sweep off in the limo to Earls Court. The concert had already started. We walked across the sitting out area backstage. There were little tables with umbrellas, trying to imitate a café in France or Italy. We got to our box. The concert was at full deafening throttle. We sat down, and after about three minutes, Yehudi said, 'This is the most terrible noise I have ever heard. I have to leave at once.'

I was not in good shape at that time, probably because of my pelvis fractures. However I saw that this was a crisis. So we escaped back through the café scene. Rupert had to stay behind. We got into the limo and went back to Holland Park, where there was a large crowd of press reporters sitting on our doorsteps waiting. Yehudi was not surprised and I imagined that he must have invited them. I opened the door and they all flooded in and followed Yehudi into the drawing room. I rapidly said goodnight. He was too busy to notice and so I went thankfully to bed. Next day several of the top newspapers were full of what Yehudi had thought of the Stones, which, suffice to say, was not much. There was not a word written about the generous donation that they had made to his school. Some years later, Rupert told this story to Yehudi's daughter. She said she thought it typical of her father.

* * *

We were in a V.I.P. lounge in a London Airport. We were on our way to a glittering three-day wedding event in Germany.

I was musing about the hideousness of the lounge décor to my husband: it was an aggressive gingery brown trimmed in orange. Freezing jets of air-conditioning bore down on our shoulders. Two pristine girls in uniforms glided noiselessly round. They smiled engagingly, ready to flirt lightly with the various businessmen.

In the midst of all of this, we could not help noticing a tall elegant middle-eastern looking young man of about twenty-eight. He seemed to be constantly drawing attention to himself with a clear, loud voice and German accent. He had large, dark and elongated eyes – like those of the figures on an Egyptian frieze – and black curly hair. Altogether, he had a certain beauty. He was, apart from a dark navy blazer, dressed entirely in Gucci. He came up behind our banquette and started a series of important sounding telephone calls, conducted in various languages.

Once on the plane, which was half empty, we saw that he had the aisle seat across from us. I fumbled distractedly with my seat belt. The young man immediately leant over and asked if he could assist me. A few minutes later he leant over again and enquired whether we were going to the same wedding as him. This we affirmed.

'I have a limousine in Munich,' he said. 'Would you accept a lift?'

We declined as an old friend of ours had hired a cheap car and was waiting to pick us up.

At the pre-wedding ball the young man, an Israeli, made the very best of the evening.

About a week after returning to London, my husband was surprised to receive a florid letter from him asking permission to take me out to lunch. This person already more than intrigued us both.

I met him at the Connaught Hotel. He was dressed in a tweed suit, with a bright yellow cashmere cardigan of the highest quality. The lunch was a great success. We were still at the table at 4.30. I was surprised by his almost uncanny intuition about people and situations and his rare, subtle, sense of humour. He understood thoroughly the mind of the Jewish people and also had the capacity to laugh at himself and all the strange problems that faced him. He told me that when he first came to London he was very overweight: that he drank, smoked, wore affected clothes such as an ankle length tweed overcoat and carried a fancy walking stick. The only person he knew well was a West End hairdresser. After seeing an excellent psychotherapist, he lost weight, learnt to drive, gave up smoking and took to espressos instead. He was ready to conquer London.

After this the invitations fell thick and fast. The middle eastern gentleman lived in a large over-heated flat in an unfashionable West End square. It was full of suspect French impressionists and Picassos. The décor was mostly pink and brown. The dining room table was made of glass and lilies and orchids were underneath it. Ballet music was generally played during lunch and dinner parties. Quite often the wrong sort of wine was served. I remember that he once served port to me with the main course. He did not drink alcohol himself.

Once, on walking down the passage to a lapis lazuli bathroom with gold taps, I glimpsed his bedroom – a large and brightly lit room with a round bed covered by a mink rug with a large stuffed toy monkey placed in the middle. The ceiling was entirely mirrored.

The Israeli rapidly became obsessed with me. He felt that I had everything that he wished to possess.

Love letters began raining down on me, often covered with stick on red hearts. Flowers and small discreet presents, including photographs of himself, arrived. His Bentley and chauffeur were always at my disposal. He was an excellent escort: reliable, punctual and with the ability to make a woman feel really worshipped. He quite often arrived in a low roaring Porsche sports car which I was afraid of not being able to get in and out of quickly enough.

I was at least twenty years older than him. He telephoned me incessantly from all over the world, day and night. I was delighted by the attention and my husband was highly amused and looked forward to the next bulletin whenever he got back from his business trips.

The Israeli met many important people at their various houses and asked them back to dinner parties and various other entertainments. His guest list began to improve, his servants became more superior and nearly all of his former friends were dropped. His thoughts began to turn to moving home. He bought part of a beautiful house in Hyde Park Gardens.

He had by now made friends with Hubert de Givenchy and Alexis de Redé. They both assisted and advised in refurbishing the glorious house. After that there was no holding him back. It was said that he once had three dukes at his table, two of them not on speaking terms with each other. I had warned him of this but it had fallen on deaf ears. By this time he was well away.

I noticed several new guests of note at his evening parties. I asked him where he had met them. He said that there had been a blizzard at Geneva airport and fog at another airport during the winter and that he had met them all or perhaps more accurately, picked them all up, in VIP lounges. There were duchesses, archduchesses, princes and a pair of small rather good-looking foreign Royals. That was a real catch.

Maria Theodora, known as Dora, was our daughter and youngest child. I remember one day, when she was seated at the kitchen table. Her feet dangled down from the chair and she wore bedroom slippers with rabbits' faces on the front of them and a pink quilted dressing gown. She had tied a spotted bandanna around her head with a huge bow on top. I came into the kitchen and sat down next to her. I was dressed in a straight black dress and was wearing a long rope of pearls. I put my open bag on the floor.

'Mum?'

'Yes.'

'Where are you going?'

'I'm going out with the Israeli.'

'Oh, not again, you know I told you he is only after you for social advancement.'

'I don't think entirely – you're so cruel.'

'Don't say I didn't warn you.'

Dora looked at me protectively but strictly. Her cheeks were bright pink and she had blazing blue eyes and a very cross expression on her face, thinking of the Israeli.

'Why can't you just stay in and look at telly with me?' she said.

'Well, the Israeli has a friend he wants me to meet, a Mr Montefiori,' I replied.

'What a name.' she groaned.

Lowering her eyes, Dora saw the Dachshund puppy prising my cheque book out of my handbag on the floor and hurrying away down the passage. She did not immediately say anything as she was so put out by the Israeli business. After a minute or two, she finally brought the incident to my attention.

'Maxwell has got your cheque book Mum.'

'What?' I said, leaping to my feet.

Dora was before me, and hurled herself after him. There was a wild struggle. He had extremely strong jaws and always held on to anything that he particularly liked.

'Better let him have it, it's too torn now.'

'Mum, do you want a drink?'

'Oh, do mix me a very small vodka with ice, sweetheart.'

Dora hopped to the drinks tray, bringing back a full tumbler of neat vodka.

'What on earth?'

'You know you'll drink it.'

'I couldn't possibly, not all of it.'

'I do need a drink,' I thought, 'to get in and out of that Porsche.'

'Eez ready!' called Pieretta, the Italian cook.

'Thanks Pieretta,' replied Dora, as she sat down in front of a plate of baked beans with fish fingers on top.

'Night Mum, and don't be late.'

'Goodnight sweetheart,' I said.

As I went out I gave a dark look at Maxwell who was seated in my special armchair in front of the TV, ready for the evening – and with the cheque book tucked firmly under his chest.

Luckily the Bentley was below. The air-conditioning meant that it was freezing. The chauffeur was a rather disagreeable old Yorkshireman stuffed into a dark uniform. He was called Baxter. One was lucky to get an answer out of him.

We headed in a different direction to the one I expected.

'Where are we going Baxter?' I yelled.

(He was also deaf.)

There was silence. So I tried again. He finally heard.

'Sir is at the sun parlour Madam. We are picking him up there,' he growled in his heavy accent.

The Israeli slid into the Bentley, grinning from ear to ear, in an open white silk shirt and perfect dark blue suit. His tie was in his pocket, ready to put on. Compliments flowed over me.

'You will find Dante Montefiori a very beautiful human being,' he said.

'What does he do?' I asked.

'He is a jeweler,' he replied.

'How that man stinks,' he said, about the chauffeur in French. 'I'm sure he never has a bath.'

'I daresay not,' I said distractedly, for I was thinking about my daughter's advice. Anyhow, I didn't really care about being taken for a ride. The ride was such a lovely one: rich, exciting, and glamorous. Why not? Soon I would be old.

We had a happy dinner at a Soho restaurant on the first floor with the windows open, as it was an unusually hot and balmy evening. I felt that we could have been anywhere in the world, it was all so different and exotic.

Mr Montefiori was even taller and more elegant than the Israeli, but hardly spoke.

I wondered about him. 'Perhaps he is his boyfriend,' I thought. Anything seemed possible.

I got back to the flat at about midnight and Dora was fast asleep. The chequebook lay strewn along the passage. Maxwell was also asleep on his bead cushion, lying on his back with his legs in the air. His tail thumped slightly as I passed him.

One day, whilst having lunch with the Israeli, he announced to me that he was to marry. He said that he had decided on a young girl of his own nationality and background, which I thought was an intelligent idea. He invited all of his new friends to Tel Aviv for the wedding celebrations and we duly went and had a wonderful time.

By this time the parties at his new house were of unparalleled grandeur. Every detail was attended to. The china and silver was rare and priceless. Great bronzes appeared in each room and even a small Botticelli hung in a dark corner of the hall. All the new friends flocked to these entertainments and everyone dressed in their best.

The Israeli's specialities were birthdays and christenings. A gossamer tent was put on the roof garden. A great many footmen were hired, along with gipsy bands, cabarets and child prodigies. Money was spent recklessly and with abandon. No one, but no one, knew where it came from. Many husbands of the fashionable ladies attending his parties made inquiries with their Swiss bankers and lawyers – but all to no avail.

* * *

One day the Israeli disappeared for a while, saying he had important business abroad. After about three weeks I got a call from him. He sounded extremely muted. 'Would you have lunch with me at home?' he asked.

It was a desperate lunch. He was deathly pale and had lost a considerable amount of weight. When the three footmen were finally out of the room, he burst into tears and said that he had had a great deal of trouble. Everything would have to be sold – the house, every stick of furniture and all the hopefully priceless pictures.

Though I had often thought that things were too good to last, I was still somewhat stunned. It is always difficult to deal with a weeping man.

I held his hand and felt a surge of pity.

'Where will you go?' I asked.

'Back to my house in Israel,' he replied.

'I will take the children to live there,' he sobbed.

His wife was not discussed as I knew that she did not care for social life and preferred to be with her family in Israel. He wept anew.

Later he had lunch with my husband and asked his advice in a roundabout way, but did not really reveal anything or come to the point. One always felt he was keeping a lot back.

We went away for a long holiday after that. On returning, my Italian friend, Cristina Cholmondeley, who lived in the same street as the Israeli, said she had seen all the furniture and possessions leaving the house in huge vans. When I had lunch at her house a week later, I saw a big 'For Sale' sign up outside of his house.

* * *

ERICA WALLACE

THE party had everything. It was thrown by a prin
the principal guest was Princess Margaret. It als
the police. . . .

The White Ball

Top left: The entrance, designed by David Milinaric.

Above: Marianne Faithfull, Mick Jagger and Cecil Beaton.

Left: Rupert greeting Princess Margaret.

Below left: The Skatalites performing.

Below: Hannelore Auersperg with Sunny Bulow.

Above left: 'They're very small and they don't drink'.
Above right: Peter Sellers and his then wife, Miranda Quarry.

We had been to a party given by Sunny and Claus Bulow in Eaton Square in July 1967. There were dinner parties beforehand and then everyone went on to the party at approximately 10.30. There was dancing and later more food.

We thought afterwards, in 1969, that we would do the same, not for any particular reason except that the sixties were full of parties.

I had an idea that I wanted the scene to be entirely of paper flowers. When I worked out the amount of people we would have to have I realised that we would need help from a decorator. Thank goodness we chose David Milinaric. I don't remember who suggested a colour theme but we decided on white as I always think everybody looks their best in white – and so they did! It took quite a while to organise, indeed at least six months. David Milinaric came up with wonderful ideas and I agreed with him on everything.

We had giant vases of marguerites everywhere. We chose the bands carefully and consulted Mick Jagger, who arranged for a group called 'Yes' to perform. They had made quite a name for themselves by then. The Skatalites, another band, also performed.

We found, when we were organising the party, that a large number of people whom we invited, asked if they could bring someone with them. Others rang up and said, 'did you know that you had forgotten to invite so and so?' Many ingenious ideas were dreamt up to try and get someone or other into the ball.

At the eleventh hour, a friend of ours, an ambassador to the Lebanon, called Sir Desmond Cochrane, rang me and said that his son had just married and was on his honeymoon. He asked whether he could bring him, along with his new daughter-in-law. 'They are very small and they don't drink!' he said, in an attempt to convince me. Anyhow, I thought that it was such a hilarious thing to say, that I immediately agreed.

The party was a resounding success. We had rather a lot of complaints of noise from the neighbours about the bands, but also some letters saying how much people had enjoyed listening to to it all. The last guests left at about eight o'clock in the morning. We were lucky in that it was the last night of a long heat wave. The next day it rained.

* * *

In the 1960s we were staying with Lord Dudley at his house in Hertfordshire, called Westwood. Peter Sellers and his family had recently moved into an ancient timbered house nearby.

Peter and his wife were invited to lunch. We had something to eat that required finger bowls of water to rinse your hands. It must have been seafood or asparagus. Peter drank the water from his bowl. We became friends quite quickly. I liked them both very much. He was, like nearly all comic actors, with the notable exception of Barry Humphries, rather dull.

As most people know he met Britt Ekland in the corridor of the Dorchester. This was sometime later. They married soon afterwards and we went to the wedding. It seemed that we were the only friends there. Everyone else were staff or work colleagues or family members.

Later we went on holiday south of Rome together.

We kept in touch through his further marriages, except the last one. It was tragic that he died so young. He had enormous talent.

* * *

When David Brooke's father died in 1984 and he became Earl of Warwick we went up to Warwick Castle to see everything. It was in the most terrible state of neglect, not having been looked after for so long. David's family had always lived in only one part of the castle and a lot of the antiques had been broken and abandoned in the stables. It was a sea of smashed Chippendale mirrors and chinoiserie and many important pieces of eastern art of great value. It was all pretty upsetting.

But David put his best foot forward and got everything going again, after a lot of hard work and frayed nerves.

On holiday with Peter and Brit Sellers.

* * *

We always loved Barry Humphries's shows and saw them from when they first came to London.

I went once with my son Konrad. We decided to take seats in the dress circle, just in case he called us up on stage, which would have been terrifying. (He did however manage to throw a gladioli into the first row of the circle.) Later my husband and I met him in California and we became good friends and saw him often. I was surprised and delighted to discover how well read he was. He was erudite and a devoted fan of my uncle Henry Green – he had read everything that he had written. He liked the surreal feeling about his books.

He always said that the audience on the whole liked to be frightened, and he achieved this at one show in Los Angeles. He had two men standing either side of the stage, in the audience, in dark glasses with ear phones placed in an intimidating manner. I asked him why he'd done that and he said very loudly in his Australian accent, 'I wanted to create an air of "MINACE"!'

It is so sad that he has hung up his wigs and dresses and we miss him very much. I hope to see him again and talk about books and films. We were once sitting separately in a completely empty cinema seeing Chekhov's *The Cherry Orchard*.

* * *

In 1970, I was on the Isle of Wight, at my father's house in the small sailing village of Bembridge. As far as I remember I was alone.

A friend who had a house near the sea whose husband was an MP rang me one day and said, 'Are you free on Saturday evening?'

I knew it was the Sailing Club ball and I didn't particularly want to go.

She said, 'Guess who is coming?'

I couldn't. 'The Prime Minister,' she continued, before asking me if I could come with them as his partner for the ball. I was excited.

We all met up at my friend's house and had drinks in the garden. Mr Heath was very genial and courtly in his white dinner jacket. I sat on his right at dinner and we talked about classical music as I knew he was a piano player and also something of a musical scholar. Luckily the piano was and still is also my hobby. After dinner we went to dance and had to walk down a passage in the marquee. The coconut matting was rucked up and so he knelt to smooth it out. It felt a bit like Sir Walter Raleigh and Queen Elizabeth.

I told my mother about it all the next day and she said, 'He always looks so wonderfully clean with that Dreft-like hair.' (Dreft was a washing powder of the day.)

'No wonder,' she added, 'he *is* the son of a lady's maid'.

* * *

In the 1980s, President Reagan wanted to meet the most important people in business and finance in Europe. An old friend of ours, Lord Weidenfeld, put forward Rupert's name. Rupert had recently broken his foot at a wedding, where the marquee had collapsed. But anyhow, with crutches and a nurse in tow, we were able to go. We had a wonderful tour of Washington, which we had never before visited. It was all immensely grand and spacious. We went out to dinner in many beautiful houses.

On the last day, we had lunch at the White House. We had met Mrs Reagan before, in Los Angeles. It was all a very memorable visit, which I wouldn't have missed for anything. The Reagans were so warm and hospitable.

* * *

We met Margaret Thatcher, who had become a great friend of President Reagan, shortly after she had left office, when we went to a dinner party with our dear friend Bebé Steinberg. She had a beautiful flat full of glorious works of art.

We arrived late due to bad traffic. We had not been told that it was a dinner for the Thatchers. On arrival the placement was in the hall. I was mortified, as I was the greatest possible fan of the former P.M. and had always longed to meet her. Anyway there they were. She had been ousted as prime minister a few weeks earlier.

Bebé led me up to her and introduced me. Mrs Thatcher looked up, neat and beautiful as ever.

'When I hear the words "prime minister", I think it's you!' I said to her.

'So do I,' she replied, laughing.

I asked what she had missed most whilst in office.

'Nature, grass, trees and the countryside,' she responded.

We had a good chat and she listened intently to everything I said, contrary to what I had expected. I had hoped that she would be sitting next to my husband at dinner, as I knew that they would have got on so well. But it was not to be.

After dinner I sat next to Denis. He was very friendly and charming. We had a long talk and he took out a small notebook and pen.

'I always carry this to write down anything interesting that people say,' he said.

'Very sensible,' I thought.

SEVEN

Eccentrics

T<small>HE RICH, FAMOUS AND BEAUTIFUL</small> are interesting enough, and all very well, but it has always been eccentrics – or those who go against the norm, or amuse one, in any way – that have fascinated me. Perhaps this is because of growing up around my mother. She was certainly the most eccentric person that I ever knew.

* * *

I was very fond of my mother's brother-in-law Henry Yorke or Green, the name under which he wrote.

I saw a great deal of him and my mother's sister just after the war. When I got into the then Sadler's Wells Ballet School he wrote me a wonderful letter, now sadly lost.

My favourite book of his was *Loving* which was made into an excellent film. I always believed that the episode of the dying butler was cribbed for *The Remains of the Day* with Anthony Hopkins.

Henry joined the fire service instead of the army or navy during the war. Afterwards, he and Aunt Dig were invited to stay with Evelyn Waugh, an old friend. They arrived on the platform to see Waugh dressed in a floor length grey overcoat, carrying a stick and wearing a grey bowler hat. At dinner on the Friday night Henry asked if he could smoke. Waugh said nothing, but stood up and left the room. They never saw him again!

A great friend of theirs was John Sutro, a strange character and a sometime film producer. He was enormously fat and had a great deal of charm. He had a wife called Gillian, who was pretty and elegant with red hair. She had a strong French accent but we never knew whether she was actually French.

John came to dinner with Dig and Henry in Wilton Place one evening. He was somewhat unbalanced and was known to have undergone electric treatment at

My Aunt Dig and my Uncle Henry.

one point in his life. The two men drank a good deal. John had one of his crises and it was so bad that my aunt had to ring 999. The ambulance arrived and John was put in a straitjacket. After they had taken him away Henry said, 'Where is John?'

'He wasn't feeling well, so he left early,' replied Aunt Dig.

'Well, its been a hard winter for all of us,' said Uncle Henry.

* * *

Sir Matthew Smith, the painter, a contemporary of Augustus John's, was a close friend of my Uncle Henry and Aunt Dig. On one of my trips back from Rome, Matthew asked my mother if he could paint me. I was rather bored by the idea but she rightly insisted on it. I was aged about twenty-one at the time.

Matthew was of medium height and very pale. He wore rimless spectacles as his sight was very bad. He was usually dressed in a three-piece pepper and salt tweed suit and a brown homburg hat. The sittings, on and off, lasted a few weeks and took place in a studio at the bottom end of Thurloe Square.

It was chaotic inside. There were pictures everywhere, some finished, some unfinished; frames propped all over the place; and a threadbare armchair, in which I sat. You had to pick your way between objects on the floor to cross the room.

The Orphan, my portrait by Sir Matthew Smith.

The first picture, like all his portraits, was in glowing colours. I had worn a pale turquoise coloured cotton dress with a yellow flowered pattern. He called the picture *The Orphan* and gave it to me.

He had a close girl-model friend called Mary Keene for many years whom I knew well. She was a great beauty and of somewhat mysterious character. She had also been a model for Augustus John.

I visited her often and we corresponded. She was married to a film producer and had a daughter called Alice, who is now also a dear friend. She inherited, through her mother, most of Matthew's estate and generously gave me another portrait that he did of me. In all there were nine portraits.

We used to go out to lunch sometimes at a restaurant nearby. I would guide him along slowly. He was kind and gentle and I think that his bad sight was an awful blow for him.

* * *

Not far from Sir Matthew Smith's studio, a friend of mine, a rather strange peer, lived in a rented, or possibly borrowed, bijou residence, off the King's Road in Chelsea. He was tall and walked neatly and furtively with his rather small head slightly craned forward. His hair was dark in a ring round his head, the front part of which was bald. He had large expressionless myopic eyes and horn-rim glasses, a long duck-like nose and practically no chin. He looked somewhat shady.

He was a dedicated hypochondriac. When anyone came to call he opened the front door cautiously and peered out from behind it, not allowing his body to get into the draught. 'Who is there?' he would ask, staring out blindly.

He used to ring me up quite a lot and sometimes took me to grand musical evenings, and once the eightieth birthday dinner of Malcolm Sargent, the conductor. The peer was a good pianist. His speciality was cocktail music, of the sort that is played in the palm courts and lobbies of hotels.

'Well dear,' he said to me one day, 'I have managed to get the Dowager (which was what he called his mother) put into a very nice old peoples' home, and I shall move into Cadogan Square.' (That was her luxurious, finely appointed flat complete with a reliable old housekeeper).

I well knew that the Dowager, though eccentric, was basically of sound mind, so started to demur.

'Oh no' he responded, 'she'll be so much happier there and will have plenty of company.'

(I knew at once that there was more in it than had so far been revealed.)

He lowered his voice.

'This is confidential dear. She has a very nice Louis XV commode and wants me to sell it for her. I told her we would probably only get £5,000 for it. My dear, she was over the moon, couldn't get over it.'

He did not telephone again for some time. Thumbing through a heavy shining catalogue from one of the leading West End auction houses, I saw a photograph of a really breathtakingly beautiful commode just by itself glowing in the middle of the page. 'That's it,' I thought. The asking price was £45,000 to £50,000. I shuddered.

The sale day came and went. The commode fetched a record £57,000.

The peer rang the day after the sale.

'I did pretty well for the Dowager,' he said, his voice quiet and gloating.

'That's wonderful,' I replied quickly 'now you'll be able to give her a really decent amount and make her life much more comfortable'

'Yes, I've already given her the £5,000 and she is, as I thought she would be, over the moon.'

* * *

The second most eccentric person I have ever encountered – the first being my mother – was an English duchess.

I first saw her long before she was a duchess in a London ballroom, in about 1947. She was more than usually tall and thin, with a beautiful small head. She seemed like some rare type of gazelle. Her face was perfectly heart-shaped and she had vivid blue eyes. Her hair was an ordinary thin brown and did nothing to deter your eye from taking in her sheer beauty, in all its aspects.

She stood unsteadily with a glass of champagne in one hand and a cigarette in the other, gazing into the distance. Her dress was a magical pale mauve chiffon and clung to her figure. I saw her later falling headlong up the stairs. I never knew her then but saw her again in a train with her husband and two spaniels about ten years later. About five years after that, we became close friends.

She was limitlessly hospitable and kind and all human beings of every size, shape, age and class were welcome at her house. She talked loudly and clearly and was very quick and intelligent. No subject was taboo, which at times could be embarrassing.

Once, the French ambassador, with whom she was not well acquainted, came down for lunch with us, arriving in a helicopter on the front lawn. The duchess had a passion, you could even say an obsession, with lists. On the conversation list for that day's lunch was circumcision.

Almost before he was seated on her right she said loudly, 'Now are you circumcised?'

There were at least twelve people at the table and silence struck.

But His Excellency was quick off the mark, 'No I am not,' he said. 'Why do you ask?'

'Well,' she responded cheerfully 'I am very interested in the subject.'

And so they discussed it thoroughly.

Her life was run entirely by strict and complicated rules. She had lists for every imaginable thing in the world, lists of friends and acquaintances (carefully divided), lists of people she had known who had been murdered or who were murderers themselves – and of course a suicide list. When any unusual happening or disaster struck she was delighted, as a new list could be started or another could be added to.

She was good at arranging flowers, but eventually, as they entertained a lot, she got bored with it all. As everyone knows, roses need their stalks crushing before being put into a vase. In order to save time, she decided to bite the stalks instead. Once, I rang and found that she had gone to the hospital.

'What happened?' I asked her, the next time we met.

'Well, I thought I had cancer,' she said. 'I found I had lumps all over my tongue, but luckily,' she raised her arms in the air, crossing her fingers, 'it was only the rose thorns.'

She fought a constant battle with her weight. She went on innumerable diets and took various raw foods to other peoples' houses in a variety of strange containers. However, when she fed her numerous dogs, she did pop bits and pieces into her mouth from their bowls. 'Absolutely delicious,' she would always say afterwards.

Another great passion of hers was to do impossible physical feats such as abseiling down high buildings, walking practically impossible distances or going on very strenuous foreign tours. When she travelled, she invariably made a medley of new friends, who were apt to turn up at any time but were always made extremely welcome, to the despair of her husband who was quite fastidious and easily bored.

A man in the nearest small town made the duchess's clothes. They were designed by him, which she was quite happy to go along with. They hovered in style between Indian, African and – sometimes – a touch of Mandarin. The materials were essentially English: viscose, nylon or polyester. There were odd drapes and flying panels in pastel shades usually worn over very full trousers. I have always been interested in dressmakers myself especially if they are cheap, good at copying and quick.

'What about your dressmaker for me?' I asked.

'Well,' replied the duchess 'he is not very good and very slow.'

Her dogs were spoilt, fierce and unreliable. One had actually caught and bitten a burglar, which was excellent. It made headlines in many newspapers. The duchess had of course quickly come downstairs in the intrepid way one would have expected of her, and witnessed the scene with proud delight.

* * *

When we lived in Hungerford, in the 1970s, we took a friend's cook. She was from

Somerset and called Mrs White.

Mrs White was quite tall and sturdy. She wore neither socks nor stockings but always plimsolls, sometimes without laces. She had short brown hair and often wore a loose blue cotton dress with short sleeves. Unbeknown to me, she was already eighty-six at the time that she started working for me. A former employer of hers told me that she was one of the very first women to go to university.

She was clever and knew a great deal about many things: particularly wildlife. She was thoroughly a country woman and her arms were covered with burns and scars. She used to pick up my son's cat by the scruff of its neck and tuck it under her arm and wander about. She was always up at dawn and used to complain that we wasted so much time in bed. 'The morning is at its most beautiful at six o'clock,' she would say.

Mrs White's cooking was the very best of English country food. The amounts she gave us were quite frugal.

'I think we need bigger helpings Mrs White,' I said to her one day.

'Well if I gave you more you'd eat it,' she responded. That was one way of looking at it, I suppose.

One day we were having drinks in the sitting-room before lunch. Mrs White suddenly appeared in the middle of the room. She spread her legs apart and flung her arms backwards. We all turned.

'What's it all about?' she said.

'What Mrs White?' I said.

'Loife' she responded, in her strong accent.

Everyone chipped in with what they thought. You never knew what was coming next.

My younger son loved cooking at this time and experimented with all sorts of drinks, often with a slice of lemon added. He used to make a lethal hot drink when we had colds. He called this 'The Boston Strangler'.

Mrs White was talking about him one day and evidently couldn't remember his name.

'Who do you mean Mrs White?' I said to her.

She responded, 'The one with the lemon.'

At one point we had mice in the house. Mrs White bought some poison and poured it into an empty Omo packet (a type of washing powder). From then on our clothes were washed in this powder.

When I went down to spend two or three months at the farmhouse, to recover from fractures and a nervous breakdown, she cooked for me and was invaluable in every possible way, as really intelligent people are.

A few years after we left Hungerford my daughter and I happened to be near the little village to which she had retired, and found her house in a row of small eighteenth century houses in the High Street. We knocked on the door and luckily we found that she was in and that the door was open. She seemed surprised and a bit muddled to see us. She was sitting at the kitchen table in a vest and cotton skirt (it was a heatwave).

There was a huge clacking kitchen clock upside down in front of her.

I put out my hand to turn it the right way up.

'Oh no,' she said, 'it only works upside down.'

* * *

One family that has become renowned for their eccentricities is the Mitford family.

I first got to know Nancy when I was staying with our friend Anna Maria Cicogna in Venice. It was a regular meeting every summer. My mother and her family had been friends with the Mitfords when they were all young. Diana Mitford was closest to my mother and aunt.

On meeting Nancy (she was known as the 'English governess of Europe') I noticed how elegant she was, in a classical and conventional way. It was soon after Dior had established 'the New Look'. She wore an ice blue silk three quarter length evening dress with full skirt and had a tiny waist, in the centre of

Nancy Mitford (second from left) and my Aunt Dig (second from right)
at a hunt ball in the 1920s.

Two of the many postcards I received from Debo Devonshire.

which there was a small bow. She immediately realised who I was. She was extremely affectionate, warm and interested, as she had known the Biddulphs so well.

She shrieked, 'Well I never thought I'd meet a Biddulph in Venice!' We all made fast friends from then on.

We went to the Rue Monsieur and to her house in Versailles many times. We also had quite a correspondence. When she became ill we had her to stay at Holland Villas Road. I gave her my elder son Rudolf's bedroom, which cannot have been comfortable. She wrote to him at Eton and said he was a 'martyr' to let her be there. He said she was a martyr to put up with the room. Nancy was always reminiscing about the martyrs.

We also once gave a party for her and the pop group, Crosby, Stills & Nash. They failed to turn up. But it didn't really seem to matter.

Towards the end of her life, when she became ill, Nancy went to a great variety of doctors. At first they were unable to diagnose her illness, later found to be cancer of the bones. She was brave and in great pain. My daughter was about five at the time and always placed some Smarties by her bed, in a little dish.

'These will certainly cure you,' she would say to her.

Nancy's novel *In Pursuit of Love* had been loosely modeled on Gaston Palewski, the love of her life. He was an important military and diplomatic figure throughout the war and an aide to General de Gaulle. He was charismatic and attractive to women. He was not good looking, but did have a formidable and considerable presence. Nancy alas, read too much into the romance and

A letter from Debo Devonshire.

therefore ended up being hurt. 'The Colonel', as he was known to the other sisters, finally married later in life. His bride, Violette, Duchesse de Talleyrand, a daughter of Anna Gould, was a princess in her own right. She looked like Nancy (but better), had a beautiful chateau and was rich. Nancy had a meeting with the Colonel before she died. I think that his decision to marry, a few years before, had been a deathly blow to her.

'Do you think the Colonel killed Nancy?' Diana Mosley asked me, after Nancy died.

'But of course I do,' I replied.

Nancy's end was a reminder that behind farce, there usually lurks tragedy.

Later, I became friends with Debo Devonshire, the youngest Mitford sister. We often exchanged amusing letters that we had received. Her funeral service, held at Chatsworth in 2014, was one of the most beautiful and moving that I have ever attended.

EIGHT

Biddestone

AFTER A WHILE, life at Holland Villas Road started to dwindle to a halt and we decided that we wanted to have our main house in the country. We were great friends with the Duke and Duchess of Beaufort – David Beaufort is my daughter's godfather – and so we started to look for a house near Badminton, but not too far away from Hungerford.

I was in poor health at that time, always with agonizing back pain. We searched and searched for the right house. Nether Lypiatt, near Stroud, was yet again for sale – it seemed to change hands at an alarming rate. We went to see it and I immediately fell for it hook, line and sinker.

'What a house!' I thought. The proportions were so beautiful and it was not too big. It was rather like a dolls house and on five floors. I was set on it.

But then my son, Konrad, came with us to see it. He is sensitive to any haunting

Biddestone Manor.

Dora eventing whilst we were at Biddestone.

and immediately felt uneasy and that it was certainly haunted. Then my husband was not in favour of buying it. However we did bid for it, but we lost to the other party. I cannot remember who they were. Later Prince and Princess Michael of Kent bought it and turned it into a veritable paradise, beautifully restored and done up and we went there many times.

Our search for a house continued and at last we settled on a 1660 manor called Biddestone, not to be confused with the beautiful Guinness House, Biddesden.

It was on a corner outside a pretty village of the same name. The house was typical of that period, with grey stone and gables. It had an exceptionally good garden with outstanding topiary, a small lake and a twenty five acre field beyond.

My daughter was delighted with it all as it is was horse country. She could continue to ride, hunt and do eventing. We moved in in 1977. I felt a kind of foreboding but put it down to my back pains.

It was my daughter's first half term out from St Mary's Ascot, where she was desperately homesick. I ordered her favourite dinner but she was unable to eat it due to paroxysms of weeping. I had a hay fever attack and before bed took an antihistamine. Neither of us woke in the night.

There was a knock on my door in the morning. Burglars had come in the night and taken silver, pictures, china and bronzes, amongst other things. It was devastating, as all people who have been burgled will know. I picked up the telephone but it was cut off. My daughter scampered over the field to the house next door to telephone the police and her father.

Chaos reigned for days. All I felt was fury and anger, as if I had been made a fool of. The burglar alarm had not been on as we had had a door to the library removed to get a desk into the very small room.

I never really got over the burglary and it certainly turned me against the house. My doctor told me a great many people sell up if that happens to them. I felt in a way that perhaps we should have done that. I was never really happy there afterwards. Luckily my husband and daughter loved it so we stayed there for about twelve years.

While at Biddestone I started having concerts in the ballroom, which had been converted by the former owners from a big barn. It could seat about one hundred people and had a stage. It was ideal. My hobby was playing the piano (classical music). I had learnt at boarding school and have continued on and off ever since.

I was at the time studying with Kendall Taylor, senior professor at the Royal College of Music. Our concerts comprised chamber music, singing and solo piano and we charged for tickets and gave the profits to charity.

* * *

Domestic help was again a problem at Biddestone. Our wonderful cook, Mrs White, said that we should try out her very young granddaughter, Susan.

This turned out to be an unmitigated disaster. She could just cook, but was muddled and untidy, often trying out a recipe over and over again and never washing anything up. The kitchen was in an uproar. She was a stunning beauty and incredibly simple and naive. I took her to task once as the kitchen was in such a state. After some thought she said, slowly and seriously in her deep Wiltshire accent, 'It could be laziness.'

Susan had an equally good looking boyfriend who we also took on for the garden. At that time I did not want them living under our roof unmarried. So we encouraged them to tie the knot. They had a daughter soon after but the marriage fell apart, almost at once.

The best person was our gardener, Mr Bradfield. He was a wonderfully wise and knowledgeable man, of the old school. He was honest, hard working and with high standards. He looked after a beautiful garden with lots of yew hedges, topiary, and a small lake.

Biddestone was certainly a haunted house. Konrad had some disagreeable

Imogen Lycett Green with Camilla and Andrew Parker Bowles.

experiences there. I felt a great sense of melancholy, especially in the night. I thought that this was perhaps because it had once been a monastery.

After the burglary, I saw an advertisement in *Country Life* for a dog trainer, a Mr Scott, who was pretty well known. I wrote and asked him if he could find a big dog who would guard the house and be a pet too. He replied that he had just the one. She was with a family but had practically killed their other dog. She was a black Great Dane, smallish for that breed, but exceptionally intelligent, very intuitive and a wonderful companion. But unfortunately she could not get on with other dogs. I bred from her and had many Danes for twenty years.

There were many good parties in the country in those years. I remember we were invited to a ball at Wilton House near Salisbury.

We gave a dinner party before. It was a truly unforgettable sight. Everyone really made a great effort with their dresses and tiaras were worn. Camilla Parker Bowles had a hairdresser at her house and we all went over to have a turn.

I remember seeing Prince Charles walking down the double cube room at Wilton with Sabrina Guinness in a beautiful red dress. It was wonderful to see a house of that stature full of well-dressed and bejewelled guests, lighting up the great rooms.

We also gave another ball, at our house, for Konrad. It was to celebrate his

Opposite page: The Green Ball

Top left: Dora and Auriol Culverwell. *Top right:* Leonora and Patrick Lichfield.

Bottom left: Anne Glenconner. *Bottom right:* Jerry Hall and Mick Jagger.

coming of age. I decided that everyone should be dressed in green. Princess Margaret said that she couldn't wear a green dress because she only wanted to wear her best dress, which was pink. She was not in a good mood. My husband said to her, 'Well then, you'll be like a rose among the thorns.' She was quite pleased with that.

The ball went marvellously. The music was good and we draped the house in green and had flares out on the terrace. The guests from far away stayed in neighbouring house parties.

My son had a seventeenth century green silk costume made with a lace collar. He looked wonderful.

We also gave a ball for Dora when she turned twenty. We chose Osterley Park

Rudolf, Dora and Konrad before Dora's ball.

Princess Margaret and Rupert at dinner before Dora's ball.

House, a former seat of the Earls of Jersey, as the venue. It is on the outskirts of London and has the most beautiful reception rooms, where one cannot drink red wine, in case it spills and stains the marble, so in addition we had a marquee.

David Milinaric designed the décor for the spiral staircase and marquee. Human figures, completely immobile in various statuesque postures, stood in alcoves descending the stairs. Some guests lightly touched them, wondering if they were real. They were surprised to get a wink in response!

NINE

All Around the World

WHEN I WAS A CHILD, holidays – when not at Ledbury – were mainly spent at Bembridge, on the Isle of Wight. When we were first married, and had little money, we also holidayed there, with my father, who was most hospitable. But I always hated going, not least because the peak of social life consisted of the annual sailing club ball, which was held in a leaky marquee (it invariably rained) and where one was served bad champagne, cold ham and wet lettuce without dressing. All of this was accompanied by the noise of a band playing very dated tunes rather badly.

The Spanish Royal Family once visited and the Niven family also lived there – and that made life a little more fun. I remember how David Niven brought his second wife to Bembridge for the first time. She was Swedish and spoke no English. She was also a great beauty. David referred to her as 'it.' They arrived on a liner from New York.

'Isn't it wonderful,' he said of Hjördis, as he introduced her to me.

And so 'it' was!

With Konrad and Rudolf.

On the beach at Bembridge.

* * *

After I was married to Rupert, each summer we used to go and stay with Johannes Thurn und Taxis. One of his many houses was on Lake Starnberg, in Germany.

Staying with Johannes was always a mixed pleasure. He was amusing and good looking but sinister – and a terrible, often malicious, tease. Our mutual friend, Hetti Auersperg usually came along as well. She had been a former girlfriend of his, but they had never married. We used to spend most of the day sitting – rather uncomfortably – by the boathouse, which was at the end of the garden, together. We would have a picnic and then go out in a motorboat.

Rupert was always easily prone to sunburn. One summer, he was particularly badly burnt, when we were staying on Lake Starnberg.

'I've got the best cream to sooth your burns,' Johannes said to him.

He quickly handed him a tube and Rupert, not noticing what it was, plastered some on. It was mustard. And of course he was in agony. This was hilariously funny for Johannes. I remember another occasion which exemplifies Johannes's sadism. There was a slippery, highly polished, spiral staircase in the castle. He gave Hetti a push and she fell down the length of the staircase. Luckily she did not hurt herself too much. She looked back at him and told us afterwards that he looked like a child, at its first sight of the Christmas tree.

One night, whilst we were staying at Lake Starnberg, Johannes drove us to dinner with a rich elderly American lady who had taken a house nearby. We found all of this very nerve-racking, not knowing how he would behave. On arriving at the American's house, we walked down a long corridor to the dining room. The hostess's little dog was trotting along beside us. Suddenly, Johannes bent down, picked the dog up and threw it against the wall. It naturally screeched and our hostess turned around with shock. Johannes just stared at her.

'I wonder what has happened to the dog?' he said.

Afterwards, at dinner, I spied a beautiful Fabergé bell by the hostess's place. While she turned away Johannes took the bell and crushed it in his fist and dropped it under the table.

I remember another occasion when we were staying with Johannes. I was expecting one of my sons and it was an unusually hot day.

'I'll take you for a spin in the boat,' Johannes said to me.

'How lovely – but only a short one,' I replied, without thinking.

'Of course,' he said.

How could I have been so silly! Naturally, he ensured that we were out for at least two hours with no cover from the sun or water to drink. Luckily I had a small towel and just managed to survive.

After dinner one evening Johannes sat down on the sofa next to a guest: a fat Jewish business man. He laid his arm across the back of the sofa and slowly

Staying with Johannes Thurn und Taxis and friends.

pressed his lighted cigar into the back of the man's dinner jacket. After a few seconds the guest leapt to his feet shouting, 'something's burning!' At the same time Johannes jumped up and cried, 'Heaven, what was that?' The poor man's jacket was ruined.

Johannes's sister Mafalda was tiny and Portuguese looking. She was very charming. One day, Wernher von Braun, the rocket scientist, was at lunch. When the coffee was served afterwards Mafalda popped a coffee bean into his tiny cup. Von Braun swallowed the coffee in one gulp and got the bean caught in his throat. He had a choking fit and had to be thumped on the back. Luckily he recovered. All of these jokes were hilarious to those that perpetrated them. But I must say that they left a nasty taste in my mouth.

* * *

During these years, my husband and I also stayed with Countess Anna Maria Cicogna every year in July. She lived in Venice, rather surprisingly not in a beautiful old palazzo – as at that time she was very rich – but in rather a modern house. The house had a lot of poky rooms, which were thickly decorated with dense and fussy murals, created by a very dear friend. The murals were extremely fanciful and they all portrayed some form of impossible carnival. They were very meticulous and detailed, but the end result was tedious. Even the lift doors were covered on both sides.

Outside there was a large and rather ugly balcony. I often felt that one could have been in Parioli, a modern district of Rome. On nights when the Countess gave a dinner party the servants, of which there were a great many, hung up a myriad of coloured paper lanterns.

The Countess herself was formidable, or rather had a very formidable manner. This was accompanied – and exaggerated – by a deep and commanding voice. Though she definitely felt herself to be an intellectual, I was not convinced. She was extremely dogmatic and did not listen to anything anybody said. If a subject came up that she did not know about, then the discussion would be quickly terminated. She had many genuinely intellectual friends, some of them quite brilliant, who saw to it that she felt equal to them, possibly to get their summer holidays in the bag. She was hospitable and loyal and did great kindnesses for people.

The Countess's appearance was immaculate, with everything matching and made of exquisitely coloured materials, that only the Italians seem to be able to produce. She always wore the same shape of shoe made especially in colours to match her outfits. She was ugly, of medium height and had a pock-marked skin.

Our great friend Marina Cicogna.

But nonetheless, she had a certain handsome chic.

When we stayed with her, we left for the Lido on the dot of eleven every morning and never waited a second for any latecomer. Occasionally we would stop on the way and pick up some celebrity, or notable person, from their hotel, to take them down to have lunch with us. The motor boat owned by the Countess was done up in her colours and the servants' liveries were made to match.

On the Lido the Countess had a large cabana. The chairs and chaise longues were white and were specially edged in her colours. She would spend the first part of the morning on a pedalo far out at sea, with an attendant male companion. He was not considered sufficiently socially acceptable to be included in any event, so he disappeared before lunch started.

At 1.20 the servants appeared from nowhere in their snowy uniforms, quickly and deftly laying a long table with a cloth under the awning. At 1.30 precisely

Marina and Anna Maria Cicogna at their house in Venice.

lunch was served. It was a full scale affair. There was always pasta with some exotic sauce, fish or meat with vegetables, cheese, salad and desert. There was red and white wine and two kinds of mineral water. The Countess's daughter Marina was nearly always there. She was small, blond and good looking, had a commanding expression and was always barking out orders and criticising everybody's appearance. In fact, if you were not beautiful, young or extremely amusing, you hadn't a hope.

At lunch the Countess placed her most important guest on her right. Often this was the VIP that we had picked up on the way to the Lido. She generally lectured to the assembled company, usually some eight or ten people, about Venetian art – for which she had an almost religious reverence – or on the current exhibitions or concerts. The guests sometimes tentatively put forward an idea, and sometimes a correction, as the Countess was by no means always right. If anyone looked as though they were about to correct her however, then an iron gaze would be directed at them, stopping them in their tracks.

The lunch lasted about forty-five minutes, as the Countess was above all an ardent and relentless sunbather. Her daughter would become very annoyed if there was not a hot creamy sauce on the table. Lunch must be 'caldo e cremoso' she used to say. This became somewhat of a joke.

In the high season Marina would walk up and down the beach, inspecting the nearby cabanas, where friends and neighbours and their guests were spread out. The point of this activity was to find some new beautiful young people to ask to dinner. A meek girl would stand behind her with a pad and pencil and various names would be barked out. Her voice reminded me of a spate of rapid gunfire. Beyond a certain number of cabanas you would not be seen or spoken to – as far as I remember a distance of ten cabanas was the social limit. These cabanas were on the right of the beach. After that you were certainly in limbo. Likewise, it was not done to bathe on the other side of the pier from this row of rarified cabanas. I once took a long brisk walk (walking was acceptable in both directions) with a smart dandified count, an old friend of the Countess's. Half way back I said, 'I must have a quick dip, I'm so hot.' Not only did he not reply but nor did he pause for a second in his quick step to regain his cabana! I had my bathe nonetheless and followed on later. I hope it did nothing to taint my reputation.

At lunch one could keep one's bathing suit on, but it had to have a glamorous cover up garment over it. Of course you had to have enough bathing suits or bikinis never to have to wear a damp one and never to lie on one of the liveried sun-beds in anything wet. In addition, your tan had to be perfect and no redness or signs of strap marks were allowed to be seen. Otherwise, one would run the gauntlet of the eyes of the other guests, filled with distaste and revulsion. Several English friends fell by the wayside on these rules, and if they were not important they would probably never be invited again. At best they would be talked about disparagingly behind their backs.

Terrifying as these standards were, one could not but marvel at the visual perfection of that ordered life. I doubt if we will ever see it again, in this grunge-like age, and I am grateful to have been a part of it.

* * *

The same Countess owned a magical palace in Libya, in a place no one may go to now. It was large, airy and elegant in the best Arab style. It was a little outside the city. The Venetian muralist had not got his hands on it. It had belonged to the Countess's father, who had had the most exquisite taste. Since his death it had been virtually untouched. The garden was large and filled with blocks of brilliant flowers – zinnias and other species in hot varied colours.

In the middle of a large terrace was a square pool of water with a little ladder

The drawing room of the Volpi house in Libya, which had belonged to Count Volpi, Anna Maria's father, who was Governor in the 1930s.

descending into it. At the other end was a pipe, which gushed out pure freezing cold water. The heat was intense. The sky was a brilliant, dark and steady blue. We sat around the pool in basket chairs. In the early morning the muezzin sounded, like the cry of a strange bird. It was still real in those days and did not have the metallic ring of the electronic one of today.

During the visit we went on various expeditions. These were far flung and started early in the morning. As in Venice, the right clothes had to be worn and hair had to be neatly done in the fashion of the day. It took some time to get ready. On one occasion, I left my turquoise linen dress on a chair, ready to wear in the morning. As I reached for it, to put it on, I noticed a huge purple stripe down the front. A ray of sun, already up and powerful had shone on it. 'Oh,' I thought in horror, 'there must be synthetic fibres in it.' I quickly switched to a white sun dress in the nick of time.

The Countess's daughter had arrived the night before, bringing a very young and sinister looking dark haired girl and her brother with her. They did not seem to speak any known language and so therefore they were silent – and we felt no need to talk to them.

We got into a large Landrover and, since we were six, we filled it completely. I thought to myself that it would be so lovely to have a picnic, but seeing no room in the car, imagined that we would stop at some small restaurant on the way.

It was a long journey, but all on straight empty roads, often running alongside the desert. 'We must stop so you can feel the sand,' they said. 'It is just like face powder.' I was amazed when I poured it into my palm, it was exactly the same velvety consistency and a light golden colour – quite an amazing sensation I shall never forget.

Leptis Magna was as breathtaking as all the famous photographs we had ever seen of it. We toured about singly or in pairs, going from the burning sun into the cool shade. The extreme dryness made it quite refreshing. Towards 2 p.m. we turned a corner on to what had been a stage in ancient times. With the vast tiered auditorium rising steeply behind us we faced a row of magnificent carved columns through which we saw the vast panorama and waves of the sea. It was one of the high points of my life. But more surprising still was that in the middle of the stage there was a table laid for lunch. It was complete with white cloth, glass, silver and four footmen. How had it got there? Of course another Landrover had been sent long in advance to prepare it all. It was an unforgettable experience, all the more so for being completely unexpected.

I looked up and saw a high carved, but crumbling archway in the distance. On top of this vast arch, seemingly minute by comparison, was a single Arab, wearing a turban, sitting crossed legged and watching us.

* * *

One year afterwards, we went to Rome for Easter. Marina Cicogna arrived in her car on Saturday to take us to the country for lunch. The car was tightly packed with her girlfriend, piles of luggage and a very pretty small white dog. We got in the back. Marina was always dressed in the height of fashion, and only saw the most fashionable people of the moment.

On this day, though the temperature was about seventy degrees, she wore a thick navy pinstripe suit with a very thin cashmere shawl-like scarf wound carefully round her neck. This was known as a shatouche. Anyone that was anyone had to be wearing one of these at this time.

The journey took an inconceivably long time because it was Easter Saturday and exceptionally fine. We got stuck in a narrow exit, which led off the motorway, in heavy and static traffic. Marina wound down her window and accused a driver of trying to pass her. She was always ready for a flaming row with anybody. He rightly replied that he was innocent of any wrongdoing. She then opened the door

The lone Arab on the archway in Tripoli, sketched by my friend
Michael Dillon from a photograph.

of the car on either side to prevent anyone from passing.

After this issue had been resolved, we crept on and eventually arrived at the
gates of a property on the edge of a honey-coloured village. This house had the
attractive attribute of being a town house on one side and a country house on

the other side. Its garden was delightful. Up a little drive the gates opened on to a parterre. The house lay beyond with a wide terrace in front of it and a balcony above, where we were to have lunch. The gate was opened by two young men dressed as ruffians, with torn jeans, ripped patterned jumpers, dirty trainers, long hair and beards. One turned out to be a secretary and the other personal assistant to our host.

On reaching the terrace we discovered a long table with about ten people seated around it. They all had their shatouches casually thrown around their necks.

This house belonged to the former boyfriend of a famous dress designer, who was also present. The host was neatly dressed in caramel coloured trousers, a spotless white shirt and his shatouche. The great designer himself was a very dark type of Italian. In addition to this he had a mahogany tan – and so his shining face looked to be made of wood. He had been somewhat of a beauty, but his looks were now on the wane. He had a sore throat, which he immediately announced. He was wearing several layers of clothing consisting of T-shirts and various cashmere sweaters in shades of pink. He wore a pained, invalided expression throughout lunch, and seemed unable to speak to us much.

The other guests, none of whom we knew, were all dressed basically as tramps. There was no way of distinguishing them from the young men that had opened the gate.

I asked to go to the bathroom, in order to see the decoration of the house. It had clearly been done up by a top decorator. There was not a square inch that was not marbled, dragged, stippled or hand-painted with flowers and designs. And then there was a myriad of wall papers and patterned carpets. I looked around as long as I dared and, feeling rather dizzy, regained the terrace. The only people smartly dressed were the orthodox Italian servants: the neatness of their black liveries was matched only by their expertise.

We had lunch on the balcony with an awning overhead. It was terrifically hot but still the shatouches were not removed. The tramps were on the whole good company and one of them was quite a wit. Another turned out to be a cousin of mine by marriage. He had a business trying to sell his own wine, grown on his nearby estate. He had had a well-known painter to make a label for the bottles – this was extremely pretty and original but I suspected that it had been expensive and that the quality of the wine had therefore suffered. I'm afraid that it was undeniably gut rot, which actually he freely admitted.

Afterwards, we looked around the garden. On one side a high hill rose up with a handsome castle perched on top, and on the right was a dense green wood. It had a charming dovecote and pavilion and a cool pond.

Our friend was motoring on to Monte Carlo the next day so we left in a hired car and sped back to Rome.

* * *

A few days afterwards, we arrived for lunch at a palazzo, one of the biggest in Rome – full of treasures and untouched for generations. We were a little early and there was no sign of life. We rang and knocked at several doors. Eventually a Moroccan appeared and led us to a minute, coffin-like lift. I tried to explain to him that I suffered from claustrophobia and asked whether there was another route. He did not seem to speak any known language and so at first he did not understand. But then I pointed through a window to the grand staircase and eventually the penny dropped and he went indoors again and after five minutes reappeared on the other side of the glass door, which he was unable to open. After clumsily wrestling with it for a while, a liveried and white-gloved servant of the old school arrived and opened the door instantly. He greeted us and bowed respectfully.

We sailed up the wide, shallow marble stairs and entered a vast hall with statues. Then we walked through six lofty, damask covered state rooms hung with masterpieces by Rembrandt, Botticelli and Rubens. There were cabinets of all kinds, priceless furniture and beautiful desks. There was also a music room with velvet covered walls and a high sea of chandeliers, as far as the eye could see. In the far distance were one or two people on the edge of what turned out to be a chapel.

We had not seen our hostess for about twenty years and by this point in her life she had become paralysed. She lay in a kind of wicker carriage, half sitting, half lying, pushed by a plain, powerful looking spinster cousin. I was reminded of the Queen of Spades. A private Easter Mass was being said by an archbishop in the old rite. He was of course in full regalia: glowing scarlet robes and white lace.

The Mass was nearly over so we stood quietly on the edge of the group, which consisted of about twenty people. It seemed to be a scene straight from the eighteenth century, even earlier maybe. It was just that the clothes were different. The Principessa Pallavicini was wheeled out and we greeted her. The Archbishop followed and bowed and smiled at everyone from side to side.

Drinks were handed round on silver salvers by several liveried footmen, helped by the two Moroccans in black suits. The drinks consisted of orange juice, cheap white wine, mineral water and tiny thimbles of dark brown sherry.

There were at least four distinguished silver-haired ambassadors of great charm and intelligence present that day. We saw quite a few old friends from the past. The ladies were, without exception, in silk dresses and court shoes unchanged since I had lived there in 1950. The gentlemen wore either smart grey suits or dark suits with silk shirts and ties.

We moved into a central room for a buffet lunch set on a big circular central table. The vividly painted ceiling was immensely high and this gave a feeling of great grandeur. There were four tables of eight with little gold chairs. The Principessa had her own table with the Archbishop and six close friends. An old retainer fed her tenderly whilst her twisted hands lay uselessly on a silk coverlet.

After helping ourselves to the first and main courses the Archbishop was presented with a large silver Easter egg and told to open it. A footman, accompanied by little cries of excitement from the elderly ladies, assisted him. Inside was something square and white. As His Eminence picked it up he smiled more broadly and bowed towards the Principessa. I asked my husband what he thought was happening. 'It is La Busta of course,' he said. It was always the custom to present high members of the Church with a fat cheque in an envelope, for their assistance on festive occasions.

We said a grateful goodbye to our kindly Principessa and walked back through the many salons. Other guests also left. They also decided not to go in the lift and one lady told us a dramatic story that it had got stuck once when she had been to a party there before. The Moroccan accompanied us down the staircase but was again unable to open the door. The guests, as always with Italians, struck up a deafening chorus of laughter, shrill comments and alarmist remarks, but calmed down when the senior servant reappeared and let us out into the warm sunshine.

* * *

At around this time, we were lucky to be invited on a cruise to the Greek Islands and North Africa on the *Gaviota*, which had been owned by a rich Chilean called Arturo Lopez, who had recently died. Our great friend Alexis de Redé was his long-time companion and had inherited the yacht.

Most of the guests were elegant European café society, based in Paris and sometime in Neuilly. We knew most of them but I found them to be extremely dull and limited. I was dreading being trapped with them for so long. The boat was immaculate, with a crew of twenty-two. Many of the cabins had signed French furniture and were beautifully decorated with wallpapers. They had bathrooms for everyone.

We arrived before the others. I knew the other ladies would all be in haute couture – and so they were. One south American lady boarded with huge trunks filled with every kind of long dinner dress – from Balmain to Dior – of the greatest beauty. It was black tie for dinner every night on the deck, and we changed clothes at least three or four times a day.

I was thrilled to see North Africa again and the little low white domed houses. We landed at Hammamet and went sightseeing and into the interior. We also went to Tunis. It was July or August – and so the heat was pretty intense.

Then, we went on to Greece and landed at several islands including Kos and Amorgos, the latter having no transport except for donkeys. They were waiting in a little huddle by the water side. We got onto one each and started the rocky ascent. It took some time but it was worth it. The views were panoramic: the blazing sun and endless blue sea and sky were more wonderful than words can say.

The standard of clothes – not to mention the food – was so high that I found that it drained one's energy somewhat. I would much rather have spent more time sightseeing and had a simpler time.

* * *

Afterwards, we decided to go on a trip to India. This was just before the Maharajas had their privy purses taken away. We travelled with our great friend, David Brooke (later Lord Warwick) who had already been and so knew the ropes.

We started in Bombay at a lovely hotel for two days. We went to the beach where there were little groups of poor men and children doing tricks and little acts to entertain. The sea was a sluggish blue. The heat was considerable. We travelled by plane everywhere and I seem to remember that no flights were less than six hours late. It certainly taught me never to fret again about planes being delayed.

I remember one time, our plane landed in the middle of nowhere, supposedly to refuel, but then did not start again. A group of small school children with a teacher crossed the tarmac with great excitement to examine the aircraft. They were then photographed in their group in front of it. At the same time, I saw our luggage being wheeled away into the distance. I rushed after it and told the porters to reload it. At last we took off to our destination. The stewardess, dressed in a sari, went to the back of the plane, lay down on a mattress and went to sleep. At last, late at night, we landed and had to drive a considerable way to the great palace we were staying in.

We knew the Maharaja of Jodhpur from Oxford, where he had studied for a time. He was a small man, efficient in character, newly-married and very interested in politics. We were ushered into a vast and splendidly gilded reception hall. We had mistakenly brought a bottle of whisky as a present. This was obviously not the done thing at all and very quickly it was tidied away by an underling. Everyone was welcoming and hospitable.

My bedroom was enormous. The bed was pretty well in the centre of the room, but as a central decoration there was a table with a three bar electric fire on it. I saw on a glance that the sheets had not been changed. When I mentioned this to one of the servants, he assured me proudly that the former guests had been Rothschilds.

There was a big dinner party. The food was the best we had in India. We ate with our fingers from small solid gold bowls. There were endless delicious dishes served by a myriad of fantastically robed servants, clad in turbans and wearing swords. By this time we were exhausted. The meals were always very long, but when everybody rose from the table it was over and you could go to bed. I had hoped to have a bath but only a rusty drip came out of the tap.

I asked for breakfast at 8.30. The servants came, all six of them, magnificently robed, pushing a trolley with last night's dinner napkins laid on the trays. There were cornflakes and a jug of boiled milk with skin on the top. I forget what else. I knew I could not eat that and felt the horror and alert presence of the six attendants, lined up against the wall in front of me, watching me eat my breakfast.

Rupert with the Maharaja of Jodhpur.

Touching the imprints of the women who committed suttee at the old fort in Jodhpur.

David Brooke, on the floor below, told me he did have some water coming out of his taps. I arranged, hoping not to get lost, to go down and have a quick bath. While in his bathroom (with the door locked) the Maharajah came into his bedroom to chat to him. I was stuck in there for forty-five minutes at least.

We went out for a picnic lunch in search of panthers. This was rather dangerous but the entourage was heavily armed. We saw some tracks but that was all. We sat on rugs on huge flat stones. We reached home later and found a concert about to start in our honour. There was about two hours of twanging and squeaking and having to sit very upright on thrones. I think we had three days there. Once, I attempted to walk out into the garden but there were a great many huge doors guarded by sentries, presenting arms every time you passed.

We took another smaller plane to Jaipur. This was also late. The next palace was a large Sunningdale type villa set in perfect lawns and huge beds of pansies. Here the sheets were clean but the baths and basins were not, and had black rings around them. I rang to ask if they could be cleaned but was told with a lot of bowing and smiling that it was not possible. I think that it was a rule that the untouchables did that sort of work and it seemed that they were not available. Looking under the bed I found heaps of rubbish, cigarette boxes and papers. The carpets were heavy pile and had not been cleaned recently.

The Maharani was not there as she had been taken ill suddenly with appendicitis. Her son was most kind and ordered steam pudding for our lunch on the lawn. The temperature was well over ninety degrees.

All this time we did a lot of sightseeing, then progressed to another palace, which had been built in the 1920s. It was the biggest of them all. The interior was art nouveau mainly. There were apologies as the Maharajah was away at the time.

'So I am afraid we only have a skeleton staff of two hundred and fifty,' said one of his entourage, who greeted us.

This palace was right in the desert and devoid of any greenery. There was a huge empty swimming pool in the basement and also a remarkable collection of important guns – antique and modern.

One of the most beautiful sights in India was the Mehrengarh Fort in Jodhpur. At its entrance was a slab with the hand imprints of the wives who had committed *suttee*, which was throwing themselves on the funeral pyre if their husbands had died before them. The drive up into the fort curved round several times. There were wonderful artefacts inside. The rocking cradles for the babies were the most beautiful, all decorated with gold and mirrors and swinging on ropes.

We were keen to see Jaisalmer and so we took a car five hours into the desert. The city was like a mirage, built of pale yellow stone and carved like lace. The palace was somewhat run down but had clearly once been very splendid. There was silver furniture in the drawing room with hens on most of the chairs and goats wandering freely around.

The Marahajah was small and dapper with slicked back hair like patent leather. He wore a smart dark pinstripe suit, shirt and tie and held a long cigarette

The Umaid Bhawan Palace, in Jodhpur.

holder. Later we were shown to his guest house to rest and eat something before driving back.

Eventually we returned to the Oberoi Hotel in Delhi. The comfort and cleanliness were an unbelievable relief. I peered out of my room in the skyscraper and saw a lovely swimming pool below, completely deserted, encircled with tables and umbrellas. I decided to go down and have a swim. I ordered a club sandwich and was sitting peacefully when an enormous bird, probably a buzzard, dive-bombed from the top floor of the hotel and swept up my sandwich. It must have had a wingspan of about ten feet. I was shocked out of my wits and beat a hasty retreat indoors.

One evening we went for drinks with an impoverished Maharajah, whom my husband had known years before in England. He lived in a block of flats in the suburbs. On leaving, it was very badly lit outside and Rupert fell into a monsoon ditch of about six feet deep. He dislocated his shoulder and passed out. With the help of David Brooke, who luckily was with us, and of the taxi driver, he was hauled out. But he was not in very good shape. Luckily David managed to put his shoulder back. In the future it was to dislocate on a regular basis, sometimes needing hospital treatment.

The beauty of India is something that stays with me always. The colours of the saris, the clear warm light, the myriad of wonderfully coloured birds swooping about and the monkeys chattering in trees and on bridges remain particularly strong memories. Sadly there were lots of beggars, some very persistent and aggressive.

* * *

In the early 1970s, one March, we also planned a trip to Russia. President Brezhnev was in power at that time. An old Russian friend of my mother-in-law's was to accompany us as a guide. He was already quite old and frail and called George St George. He was a great wit and very knowledgeable and cultivated.

Russia was, at that time, restrictive – as to moving about – and everyone was carefully watched and monitored. You were also not allowed to choose your hotel. Luckily we were put in the old National Hotel overlooking Red Square. Two close friends were with us. Since it was March we thought it would not be too cold. What a shock we got!

As we walked out of the airport it was twenty-five degrees below zero. Luckily, we had brought plenty of warm clothes – as had one of our friends, but not the other one, who was soon in trouble. On reaching the hotel we were shown to our rooms. They were all spacious and old fashioned. A woman guard sat at a table at the end of our passage. We had an enormous sitting room with a parquet floor. This was bare except for a huge grand piano in the centre. On seeing this I was delighted – as I am a pianist – and so lifted the lid, only to find that it was empty inside.

The bedroom was small, with just enough room for the bed. There was a tiny bathroom – and of course no plug for the bath. Luckily we had been warned of this in England and so we had brought some with us.

I looked out of the window to behold the vastness of Red Square with high towers surrounding it with lit red stars on the top. The guards were pacing the square in their long great coats and fur hats. It was gently snowing. It was an incredible sight: full of power and menace.

We went into the spacious first floor dining room. The menu was sparse and included only about four dishes. One was chicken, which I ordered. But then I was told that it was off.

At this point a tall and powerful looking man entered the room. He had white hair and a gold hammer and sickle badge on his lapel. The room froze. This was Sergey Michalkov, an important government minister and President of the Writers' Union. We had had an introduction to him and he had come to see how we were faring. There were great long lost Russian greetings between him and George St George. He asked what we had ordered and if we had everything that we wanted. I told him about the chicken and he snapped his fingers for the waiter and said, 'bring the lady the chicken!' The waiter sped off and brought it back in a couple of minutes. He very kindly gave us tickets for the Bolshoi and invited us to his birthday party.

On the next day we set off to try and find some warm clothes for our friend, Billy Whitaker, who was travelling with us. We did this with difficulty, as if you paused on the pavement outside of a shop, a soldier immediately came up and ordered you on. Nonetheless, Billy sadly was already sickening for bronchitis and from the next day he was confined to bed with his feet hanging over the end (he was at least six feet and eight inches tall). George St George went gamely out to queue at the chemist for aspirins and then asked his brother-in-law (a doctor) to come to see him. All this was achieved with great difficulty, as there was a lack of almost everything you could think of. Also it was snowing and exceptionally cold and you had to get over all the rules and regulations while being closely watched by the guardian on the landing. And then there was a curfew from 9.30pm.

I remember one night that George St George said at dinner, 'I would love to take you to Siberia next time. I can promise you some bracing weather.' I hastened to imagine how bracing.

We were meant to be moving on to Leningrad by the night train, after about four days. But this became impossible as Billy was too ill and had to recover enough to fly home. We did a lot of sightseeing instead. I loved the Kremlin Museum and seeing all the silver sent to Ivan the Terrible by Elizabeth I, among other magnificent things. We saw Tolstoy's house, which was in Moscow: it was charming and all the children's cots and lace curtains were prettily arranged. We had to get permits to go to Zagorsk. The government did not like tourists seeing places of worship and the fervent believers, peasants and beggars.

Zagorsk was only fifteen miles away. It had a beautiful cathedral, with everything in deep snow. It was almost too cold to bear. I had a shooting stick to sit on with three legs, as my back was painful. It was at once confiscated in the museums and picture galleries. I said to George St George, 'What do you think they think it is?'

'A three barrel gun at least,' he replied.

* * *

Sergey Michalkov fetched us in the car to go to his family's dacha outside Moscow for his birthday party. The house was like a big skiing chalet. Everything was made of wood, very warm and covered with checked table cloths. There was a secretary and several servants and a cook. This would have been unheard of for ordinary people. We had a long lunch and there were many toasts. His wife was large with very black hair in a bun and a middle parting. She looked very nineteenth century. There were family portraits (they were related to the Galitzines).

After lunch three Jewish musicians played classical trios. This was surprising in view of the prevalent anti-Semitism in Russia at this time. Michalkov seemed proud of this. When we enquired he said, 'If they want to remain Jews we "encourage" them to go to Israel!'

Sergey Michalkov's two sons were both well known film directors. One of them was there. He had dark hair, horn rims and wore a velvet jacket and jabot. He looked very Chekhovian. All the family were hospitable and kind. Sergey drove us back and left us at a theatre to see a display of breathtaking national dancing and the brilliant Red Army soldiers performing all kinds of acrobatic feats.

The Bolshoi was another wonderful evening. We sat in the Minister of Culture's Box and were photographed long distance from the stage. I wanted to sit alone in the box in the interval to look at everything but that was certainly not allowed. A severe but pleasant woman in black, who was distinctly in charge, shepherded me out to the refreshment room.

* * *

Vodka was always liberally available in all the restaurants. You had a small carafe of your own in front of your plate. At first I thought it was water!

The shops were incredibly poor, worse even than ours in the war. We saw a very long queue waiting to buy oranges (or possibly one orange). A guard was stamping the people's wrists with a number so they didn't get out of line. I was most impressed by the fact that there was barely any traffic. There were no adverts and no bright neon signs – indeed it was an immense relief to see no modern hideousness, at least not in the centre of town.

Eventually Billy's condition improved and he was able to take a plane home. We took the night train to Leningrad. The station reminded me of *Anna Karenina*, as snow was falling. The train was piping hot with sealed windows. A huge woman was controlling our car. Indeed, she could equally have been a man.

It was hard to sleep because of the heat. As I remember we had some form of breakfast, which was probably not edible. We arrived in Leningrad where it was much warmer and the snow was melting. We were taken to a very different hotel in a skyscraper. They gave us the penthouse suite called 'Bluebird', which they proudly announced that Elizabeth Taylor had just occupied, while filming there.

There was no form of room service. Indeed there was no service of any kind. You had to queue at the canteen for everything. George St George kindly did this for me and brought some biscuits and tea after a very long wait.

Nonetheless, we could see Leningrad as it then was, which was beautiful, but very run down. (Since then of course it has been extensively renovated.) One regularly looked up at high elegant windows to see washing on a line. The Hermitage and other great museums were wonderful, though again shabby. There were acres of great masters. Talking was not allowed, only whispering, and there were guardians and curators in every room.

There appeared to be no restaurants for tourists. My husband had an 1850 Baedekar in which he found a recommended restaurant at Petershof. We asked the taxi driver to take us there. He refused over and over again but finally gave in. It was a really nice, old restaurant, with great atmosphere, packed with Russians only. The food was good and we felt we were seeing the authentic Russia. Most other restaurants had notices on the door saying 'closed for lunch' or 'closed for dinner'. It was all very much like something out of Kafka.

Poor George St George must have been exhausted afterwards. He died shortly after the trip. We always missed him so much.

We went again to Russia several times with The Rolling Stones and also went on a trip on our own to St Petersburg. But it was never the same as the first time, which was not comfortable, but had its own magic.

* * *

Sometime in the 1980s, Princess Margaret was finally permitted by the Queen Mother to visit Germany for the first time. Queen Elizabeth had never liked the Germans and felt that the Second World War was likely to have caused the King's early death in 1952.

After this decent interval we decided – my husband, Princess Margaret and I – to go to Frankfurt to stay with the British-born Princess of Hesse and the Rhine, known as Aunt Peg. She was an immensely warm and charming person and was, I suppose, about seventy years old at the time. We stayed at her grand shooting lodge, Wolfsgarten, near Frankfurt. This was old fashioned but comfortable and was built around a big courtyard, part of which housed a school for disabled children.

We made some interesting trips to Darmstadt and to Prince Albert's old home, Rosenau, in Coburg, a beautiful yellow castle. We went on very long excursions and packed in many hours of driving so that we could see palaces and museums. We were given the very best guides and chances to see many places not open to the public.

Aunt Peg was cultured and had an enormous knowledge of these things. We went accompanied by her nephew, Prince Moritz of Hesse, to one of his many palaces, called Schloss Fasanerie. Prince Philipp, his father, had done it up himself with magical taste, beautiful curtains and upholstery and priceless furniture.

We mostly had small dinners at home on getting back and were accompanied by the Duke of Edinburgh's sister Tiny, the Hanovers and other relations.

Aunt Peg's old dog, called Mixi, was kept tethered to a tree on the lawn with his cushion and a bowl of water. The whole atmosphere was very homely.

I think Princess Margaret's family in Germany were pleased to see her and vice-versa. There were no courtiers hovering and she was on equal terms with them and they all called her Margaret.

On the way back to London, I asked her what her plans were on returning to England.

'I shall go and see the Queen and tell her all about our trip.'

'Will she be interested?'

'Oh no!' she said in her high, clear voice.

* * *

My old friends Kapi and Filippo – from my time in Rome – once invited us to Hawaii, where they then lived some of the time. As we had never been there before it sounded exciting and we were keen to go. We chose a weekend in the 1980s and flew from Los Angeles for three nights. They had rented a little house, as Kapi no longer had any property there. The scenery as we landed was quite beautiful: it was dominated by huge, green mountains. Duccio, Kapi and Filippo's son, who was then in his twenties, was there. He was handsome and tall with formal manners.

None of them could cook so we did not have any meals in the house. The kitchen was dark brown. On the first morning, they asked us what we would like to have for breakfast. They seemed only to have toast or cereal. Rupert always liked to have a boiled egg so having said that, they really didn't know what to do. Duccio picked up the largest cooking pot he could find and filled it to the brim with cold water. He was hardly able to lift it. I quickly suggested finding a small one instead – and duly took over the process of preparing the egg. Somehow we got it boiled, but it was rock hard in the end.

The beach was a little way down the empty road. It was not particular in any way: there was no white sand or brilliant blue sky, rather everything was grey and windy.

We sat on the sand while Duccio arranged his canoe. Afterwards he jumped in and rowed rapidly away over the horizon. When he didn't return, quite a while later, I got anxious. The others had gone back to the house to get ready to go out to lunch. At long last, when we returned from lunch, he came back.

I said how worried I'd been.

'No harm can come to me on the sea because I am royal and am protected by the Gods,' he replied.

I was impressed by the seriousness with which he said this.

We had a friend in common living there, a man from one of the great American families. He was rather distinguished looking and aged about forty-five. He had left his wife and four children – who were all young – to live with a small and comical looking old man with a little straw homburg hat perched on his head. This caused much merriment.

We had driven a long way along a traffic-laden road to find the American's house, which was somewhat indifferent. It was not quite on the sea and had a tiny garden. He and his new friend were friendly and hospitable and a great deal of drink was consumed. I think that Filippo couldn't get over this extraordinary happening and so he talked about it all the time, throughout lunch. But it was an odd way to spend a day. We didn't see any of the country except the former Royal Palace, where the family used to live, which was now open to the public.

We met Kapi's charming sister for drinks one night at one of the grandest hotels in the bay. She was of such enormous proportions, like many Hawaiians, that she travelled in an open lorry. She was almost unable to walk.

On our last evening I thought we might have gone to some local restaurant – but no, we drove a great distance to the Hilton Hotel, where we had dinner in a vast air-conditioned dining room, which was heavily chandeliered. This took an immense amount of time as the service was poor.

Filippo, when at home, sat in the kitchen in a dark corner looking at television. I preferred to see them in Spoleto and hope to still, as Duccio has now restored his palazzo. Sadly Filippo died some years ago.

He is irreplaceable.

* * *

Jimmy Goldsmith bought thousands of acres in Mexico in about 1980, a shortish flight from Puerto Vallarta. He built a Moorish – or Indian – style mansion on a high promontory overlooking the sea. It was constructed on different levels with various elaborate courtyards and a spacious sweeping staircase down to the beach below. This was punctuated with fountains playing as you walked down. It was beautiful but quite a job climbing up again. At the bottom was a large swimming pool with mosaic surrounds. At the beach level there was a round terrace with chaise longues – beside which there was a big gazebo with a thatched pointed roof where we had lunch.

The beach went as far as the eye could see in both directions. One could not swim in the sea however, as it was too dangerous and with massively high and strong waves crashing onto the beach.

We arrived at Puerto Vallarta from Los Angeles. Jimmy had sent a wonderful plane, which seated about twenty. Inside it there were lots of high windows, so you could see the scenery. The seats were covered in bright check material and were like those in the old buses in England. It had double wings and propellers. I think it took about forty-five minutes to get to his estate. Jimmy had built a village with a school, church and several houses. There was a big lake with exotic birds and, we were told, crocodiles.

We were taken to a guesthouse, which was quite far away from the main house, with a huge bedroom high up overlooking the crashing ocean. It was done up in the most exotic satins in brilliant Turkish style colours. I did not want to seem ungrateful but I felt uneasy being away from the main house, and was rather scared of scorpions and snakes sneaking in during the night!

I later discovered that Jimmy had a particular horror of scorpions too, as a guest had once been bitten. Accordingly, he had built a moat of approximately one foot wide around the house. Apparently a scorpion cannot jump so would have landed in the trench.

I spoke to Jimmy's son who at that time was running the house and he soon found us two bedrooms in the main house. The furniture was built into the floor and the beds had a rounded edge at floor level so that insects could not climb up.

There was no mention of breakfast in bed, just that it would be on an upper floor from 7.30 onwards. We went up at about eight o'clock. There were many very erudite and intellectual guests from America. When Jimmy turned up it became rather like the quiz shows on the television, on serious subjects, such as politics. Jimmy held forth and was always interesting. Then everyone in turn was asked their opinion. Before they got to me I made my escape as there was no subject on which I was particularly knowledgeable. After breakfast we were all assembled, as there was to be a tour of the immediate property. We suddenly heard several gun shots.

'Whatever is that?' I said.

'Oh, they are just dealing with the poachers,' Jimmy replied casually.

It was rather a shock. But as the property was so well fortified, he felt that it was justified.

One of his guests from an earlier house party told me that when he was taking a walk down the beach before breakfast he found a dead body. He rushed back to the house in a great state and told the butler.

'I'm so sorry sir, I have not had time to clear it away yet,' he replied.

We had a tour around the estate, which was fascinating and included the horses and stables and a boat-ride on the lake. The next day we were taken by car to a small private cove, where you could swim. It was all set out with chairs and a picnic pavilion.

* * *

My friends Elizabeth and Mark Dent-Brocklehurst, David Brooke and I once went on a Kuoni tour to Thailand. The Brocklehursts and I flew directly to Bangkok. The hotel was quite nice, as I remember. At any rate it was clean. We were joined by David, who had come from Burma, and we went on some Kuoni tours. The temperature was 125° in the shade. We saw a lot of golden temples and endless Buddhas. Bangkok was a sea of noisy traffic, rickshaws and long roads with gimcrack buildings going for miles.

We had an interesting contact through Rupert's Uncle Hubertus to Princess Chumphot, who was the King's aunt. We were invited to tea. She sat on a kind of throne barking out orders to the servants, who had to come into the salon on their knees and departed on their knees backwards, as they had to face her at all times. There were several other Thai people there and so it was rather like an audience. The Princess was very sharp, formidable and unapproachable. It was an interesting peep into the royal world.

* * *

We were once staying in our house in Los Angeles for a couple of weeks. I had my old friend Margaret-Anne Stuart staying too.

We had never been to Las Vegas and longed to go. But as Rupert had been several times already he didn't particularly want to go again. A friend of ours, a young and leading promoter called Andy Hewitt, kindly asked us to go with him and his girlfriend in a private plane. He said that he would treat us to the hotel. We were going to a Stones concert the first night, and the Cirque de Soleil 'O' (or Eau), the next night.

It was a quick flight and we arrived at the MGM Grand Hotel. The lobby was vast and, further on, a sea of slot machines could be seen.

Checking in was not easy. Andy had booked us into an attic suite, which was the most fashionable part of the hotel. We sailed up in one of a mass of gilded lifts. We walked down what seemed like miles of carpeted corridors coming now and then to a crossroads, where smart girls sat at desks. I had long ago lost any sense of direction. Eventually we came to our crossroads where some very elegant black girls, like models, and dressed in pale grey, were sitting. We went along one final corridor and then we were there.

On coming into our suite we found a hall, two huge bedrooms with heavily over upholstered beds covered in a mass of scatter cushions and a bedspread, which was too heavy to lift off. Above all, everything was electronic – powered by gadgets and buttons everywhere. We were given a tour and told how everything worked, but it was not easy to take in.

A young Englishman appeared and introduced himself as our personal butler, available to serve us at any time. He led me into the bathroom. This was a huge marble room. The enormous bath was surrounded by a deep marble surround and was full to the brim with water.

'I've already run your bath for you,' he said. This seemed a little bizarre, and I wondered how he could have known whether I had wanted a bath or not. After prostrating myself over the deep surround, I dipped my hand in. The water was stone cold. Margaret-Anne luckily had a smaller bath, in a more manageable bathroom.

The butler – who was from Liverpool – said we must call him at any time. When we tried to do this there was no answer and we never saw him again.

The Stones' performance was the usual concert and I took Margaret-Anne backstage and we had a chat with everyone. The Cirque de Soleil 'O' or 'Eau' was a dream with the amazing acrobatics, a lot of which took place over and in water. Dancers floated in mid air in eighteenth century costume. It was all a really fabulous display. Andy had arranged for two glasses of vodka to be passed down to us in the stalls. These were most welcome.

After the Stones concert we got back to the suite. I went into my bedroom and the door clicked shut. Margaret-Anne came along to chat and couldn't open the door, as it had triggered its burglar lock. This took some time to unravel. She could not find out how to turn off her bedside lamps either and so had to sleep with them on all night.

Our breakfast was enough for about twenty people. Apart from all these hazards, we did enjoy it very much.

* * *

These days, I do not travel too much. But there is still one place that can tempt me away from England: an exotic, paradisiacal and calm island in the West Indies.

It is called Mustique.

TEN

Mustique

I HAVE ALWAYS BEEN A SUN WORSHIPPER and have had an obsession with sun ever since I was about twelve years old and living with my grandparents at Ledbury Park. A cousin gave me an expensive sundress, which I set about, with help, cutting up into two bikinis. From then on, whenever there was even a hint or a glint of a ray of sun, I would lie flat on the lawn directly in front of the old dining room, which during wartime was full of ladies working for the Red Cross making clothing for the wounded. When allowed, I did of course help with this work.

Years later, craving the sun as usual, we went to stay with Colin Tennant, a distant relation of mine, who had acquired what I suppose one could call a paradise island. It was the late 1960s.

Colin was a highly volatile character. He was full of fantasy and outstanding wit and was talented in many fields. He was blessed with charm in abundance and good looks. In a way he waved a magic wand over the island, which was practically uninhabited when he bought it. Colin began developing it, creating a new village for its inhabitants, planting coconut palms and fruit trees and building homes for his friends.

When Princess Margaret was on honeymoon in 1960 with Tony Armstrong-Jones, they visited Mustique and added an immediate element of glamour and recognition to the name of the island, up until then virtually unknown.

Colin and his wife Anne kept on asking us to Mustique, and finally we decided to go one winter in the early 1970s. The only way you could arrive there was by flying into St. Vincent and then taking a boat. Later the airport was built.

The tiny plane rocked from side to side before flopping down onto a very simple runway. The airport – although it barely merited the description – consisted of a bamboo hut with the flags of many countries flying from poles on the roof.

A tall young black official in a smart beige uniform and black-peaked cap

An old photograph of the Cotton House, Mustique, now a hotel.

slowly approached my suitcase. He tapped it with his cane.

'Yes, please, opayn,' he ordered.

His face carried all the gravity of new-found power. He searched the case with great care. Behind him on the wall was a notice declaring, 'It is forbidden to smuggle heroin, fruits or vegetables in your luggage.' In the distance, in the little customs office, I could see some odd-shaped fruits laid out in a row, doubtless confiscated from some traveller's case.

'In de clear,' he said finally, tapping the case again.

The island was still quite primitive. There were hardly any houses. Oliver Messel, a friend of my family, whom I had known since my ballet days and had seen in his artistic element as a set designer, was busy designing these new houses: the first of which had been built for the Guinness heiress, Lady Honor Svejdar.

The only original island building was the Cotton House where, as the name suggests, cotton had been produced in previous times, and which was still only one huge room. Colin had filled the space with beautiful antiques and glass cabinets containing brilliantly coloured stuffed birds, mostly from his Scottish castle, Glen. Oliver created an annexe of four bedrooms, as elegant and comfortable as I would have expected. Rupert and I were the first people to stay there.

The island remained utterly private, and daily life was like an ongoing house

Unveiling a statue of Colin Glenconner on Mustique.

party. Princess Margaret was nearly always there when we went. Colin would ring us in the morning and tell us that we were all going to have a picnic on such and such a beach or drinks in this or that house.

Alongside his generosity, Colin had a vicious and totally unpredictable temper, which once unleashed could be of alarming proportions. Any tiny detail – and you could never predict what that might be – could trigger it off. This might not happen for months, but you could never be sure when he was going to explode.

On one visit I stayed with Colin in his own house, called the Great House, a fairytale coral pavilion with a huge marble hall and a bedroom with a silver bed. There were several bamboo guest huts, Thai style, on stilts in the garden.

We went down to the harbour in a small car, essentially a motorised golf buggy, called a mule. The fishing boats were all laid on the shore in brilliant colours. The local fishermen were lying under palm trees staring up at the sky.

A large blackboard announced, 'To-day samon for sale (fish).' So we bought a large one.

When we returned to the Great House the fish was consigned to the houseman. He was given no particular instructions except that it was required for a large buffet luncheon the following day.

I saw that the fish was far too big to go into the fridge. As I did not wish (or rather did not dare) to interfere I watched spellbound as he hacked the fish into large pieces and put it in the freezer.

I was alone that evening, as Colin had business on another island. He had arranged for me to go to a cocktail party at a neighbouring house. Armed with my orthopaedic cushion (carefully covered in vivid grass green velvet by my daily) I gingerly climbed into the mule. The houseman drove wildly over the undeveloped roads. He wore a round woolly hat with a pompom on top of it. The temperature was a steady ninety degrees, even though it was evening.

The cocktail party was dull and given by a vulgar and rather lecherous host. I did not linger for long and on coming out and boarding the mule I noticed the absence of my cushion.

'The cushion must be back in the house within the hour or your master will hear of it,' I told the houseman firmly.

Back at the hut I opened my bamboo door to look at the stars before turning my light out, and there was the glaring green of the ortho cushion lying in front of my door, propped against the wall. Most things that 'disappeared' were subsequently found in the tents on the beach, including a set of brand-new banquette cushions covered in a beautiful material with grapes on, that had cost Colin a small fortune.

The next morning I awoke to the most terrible screaming and yelling I had ever heard. Luckily I was quick on the uptake. 'The fish!' I thought, as I fled out of the bamboo hut in my nightgown, knowing there was not a moment to lose.

The houseman was cowering on the kitchen floor. Colin had a long knife in his hand and was in a state of total hysteria. The fish lay in lumps, some on the formica top, the rest on the floor. Luckily my reflexes have always worked in a crisis.

I rushed up to Colin, and yelled in his face, 'Shut up!' very loudly, three times, quickly followed by a quiet, 'It's perfectly alright. We'll fit the pieces together with sellotape underneath and make a mayonnaise pattern over the top. It'll look lovely.'

Colin stopped raving at once and smiled quickly.

'What a good idea. So that's settled then,' he said.

Murals in our house on Mustique painted by Michael Dillon. They are copies of Léon
Bakst's designs for the Diaghilev ballet.

We both left the kitchen. The houseman waited on the floor for a minute or two to be sure, and then got up and went on with his work.

Sometimes Colin's children would be on the island. On one trip, his second son, Henry, was staying. He was an unusual, extremely tall (probably six feet eight inches) and willowy red-haired boy in his late teens or early twenties. Henry was a fanciful lad, charming and kindly, but very out of the ordinary. He often used to dress up in younger days in a crinoline and wig when he was in Scotland, much to the distress of his mother.

It was 'jump-up night' at the beach bar. When Colin had first bought the island, the notice over the bar's entrance had been 'Basil Bar', expensively made up in bright green neon in St. Vincent. Since then they had learned a thing or two. Sadly, I saw it had been corrected.

We tore down to the beach in a small open car with benches in the back. Colin wore a smart white outfit and his habitual straw hat. His son towered over us, likewise attired, his pale red hair blowing in the wind.

The bar was made of bamboo and stretched in a promontory over the water. Little tables were dotted all round with bright red and white check tablecloths. Colin strode in, his eyes blazing, but as yet quite friendly. He looked around, checking on all the details.

A wonderful buffet had been laid out: suckling pig, barbecued chicken, fried pumpkin and exotic salads. Two or three chefs with shining faces and tall hats stood behind the table, ready to serve. We sat down at a table and ordered drinks. The steel band twanged in a desultory way next to the small, square, concrete dance floor.

Halfway through the main course Colin stood up with his 'looking for trouble' expression on his face. 'Just a moment, there is something I have to see to,' he said.

He strode out to the bar where the manager was standing in an expensive but gaudy caftan. He was a powerfully built man with blue-black skin.

'I expect you have remembered the gateau?' Colin said in a challenging tone.

The manager looked back stony-faced as his mind slowly churned, trying to think up a suitable answer.

'I forgot, boss, but there is fruit salad, and mango.'

'I have said a thousand times that there must be a gateau on Saturday nights,' yelled Colin, already out of control. 'Because it's a gala night, man, and the guests expect a gateau, a gateau, a gateau!' he screamed. 'You are just a stupid, no good man, and don't know how to do the simplest thing properly.'

Opposite page: Our house, Zinnia, on Mustique.

The veranda at Zinnia.

Margherita and Aliotto on Mustique.

By this time Henry and I, watching from our distant table, saw that real trouble was afoot. We got up and sped to the scene. Before we could get there Colin had thrown his glass of neat vodka in the manager's face. A clutch of woolly hatted kitchen helpers rushed out from the kitchen, gathering force and closing in, ready to attack Colin. Henry quickly floated into their midst like an oversized flamingo and waved his arms in the air.

'Now Dad, come on, calm down, we're off home now.'

Colin continued to shriek unabated. Suddenly, and most unexpectedly, Henry slapped his father sharply in the face. There was complete silence for a second or two. We took him, one on each side by the arms and led him to the car. He started quietly chatting as if nothing had happened. The dinner was forgotten and we drove home.

* * *

For nine or so years we went annually to Mustique, sometimes renting houses ourselves, or on one occasion taking one with Colin when he was himself between houses. We were tempted to buy a place of our own but realised that if we bought a house, or land to build on too soon, we would never travel anywhere else.

The house we now own was built quite early on, with a centre house and two lodges on either side. It was decorated with 'gingerbreading', that traditional lacy white-painted woodwork, which one sees in the Caribbean. The central part of the house was quite small – just one bedroom and sitting room downstairs – and had no veranda around it, which meant that the rooms became extremely hot. The staircase was outside at the back, so in rainstorms you would get soaked going up to bed.

I realised that if I pulled it down and made a larger imprint, encompassing the ground at the back, then the house could have four double bedrooms with bathrooms and showers, and downstairs a large room and dining room all in one, and a curved staircase gliding up. A friend of ours, Tony Milsom, who formerly worked with Lord Linley, Princess Margaret's son, had started building on Mustique. Our house was one of the first major jobs that he took on, and Rupert said if that if he could build it in nine months he could have the job. Everything works very slowly in the West Indies, so I was somewhat sceptical. However, it was finished on the dot which was a great relief and all due to Tony's efficiency.

The house had originally been called 'Banana Bread' but I felt that was rather too 'toy town'. One of my favourite flowers is the zinnia, especially the green one called 'Envy', so we called it 'Zinnia'.

＊ ＊ ＊

Many years after we first went to Mustique, I was staying in a beautiful and very expensive hotel in Barbados. I was with my cousin Molly. Molly lived in the wilds of Scotland alone, and was always ready at the drop of a hat to go absolutely anywhere. In fact I had only suggested the trip about four days before we set off. After we arrived, we lay on the white beach enjoying every second. The sun beds were all laid out neatly every morning with spotless towels and umbrellas. The sea was an incredible brilliant-blue, with clear shades of aquamarine, and various small sailing craft flew about with lovely mauve and pink sails.

By this time, Colin had found the cost of running Mustique too much and so had handed over the island to a company. He had then bought a perfect untouched green bay dotted with incredibly tall palm trees on another much bigger island. It was an old religious site.

'I think we should visit Colin,' I said. 'We'll take a small plane and go for the day because his little house is bound to be uncomfortable.'

Colin had hoped to develop the bay himself and wanted to build a beautiful hotel, which of course he would have done better than anyone. Alas, he could not find any congenial tycoon to back the project. In the end he had had to settle for an Indian with little, if any, taste, who after a bit eased him out, and left him with a little patch at the side of the hotel, where he ran a small bar.

Molly agreed and we set off early and the little plane flew steadily through the cloudless sky. When we landed there was no sign of Colin. We wandered into the bar. There was a disagreeable old black lady hunched up behind it.

'I'll have a coke please,' I said.

'You no coke, bar eez shut,' she responded before she climbed off her stool and hobbled away through a backdoor.

I turned round to see Colin standing there smiling. He was dressed in a grubby white outfit, Indian shirt and trousers and his favourite battered straw hat. I recalled how he had chartered a plane to fly back home and fetch this hat once, when he had left it behind on a trip to Martinique.

He clasped me in his arms and was openly delighted to see me.

'He is so lonely,' I thought.

'Where's Molly?' he asked. She was peering at some postcards on a stand. Though they were distantly related they did not know each other, and I immediately felt that they would not get on. We walked outside into the blinding heat. I saw a battered truck standing in the car park and knew it must be his.

'It's quite a short drive,' he said, smiling slyly.

'What sort of short?' I asked.

'About an hour and a half,' he replied casually.

I suggested that Molly sit in the front. I got in the back where I could cling to any available handle to lessen the crashes of the truck on the unmade roads. On arrival, I saw the half constructed hotel, completely ruining the magical bay. My heart sank. Of course it was no good saying anything derogatory to Colin, knowing his violent temper. We got out to have a look, when it suddenly started pouring with rain, quickly drenching us. There were beastly little bungalows dotted all over the place, which he assured us would soon be covered in creeper. After a tour we got back into the truck. On the way back Colin suddenly stopped and threw some cigarettes to an old bent black lady, who was sweeping the little garden in front of her wooden house. She grinned conspiratorially, showing her one tooth.

'That's Miss Hanna,' he said laughing. 'She lives with an old man and if she smokes he beats her up.' He screeched with laughter. We did not reply and were naturally shocked by the sudden cruelty of his remark.

We started scaling an almost perpendicular hill. 'I can't stand this,' I said to Colin, 'I'll get out and walk.'

'Come on,' said Colin. 'It's too steep to walk, I promise you.'

I insisted and he and Molly, who hadn't noticed anything, carried on in the truck as it struggled up. It looked as if it was just about to somersault backwards.

I tackled the hill. He was right: though I was fit, it was not possible. After ten minutes waiting he came back giggling and pulled me up.

'Why on earth are you travelling with Molly?' he asked me.

'She is so easy and placid and never talks when you don't want her to,' I replied, adding 'she will go anywhere, and doesn't mind what she spends.'

'You mean it's like being alone only better?'

I laughed. 'Yes, that's what it's like.'

We finally got to his little wooden hutch house. It had a really spectacular view. A hopeless looking young black girl stood motionless over a stove. I could not see any food, or preparations for lunch. Colin, who was as usual not drinking, forgot to offer us anything.

'Well, I wouldn't say no to a drink,' I said, slightly wearily. Tepid vodka was duly produced in a tumbler. Finally, a strange and not very edible lunch was prepared. I looked at the clock and realised it was nearly time to start the bumpy ride back to the airport.

'We better go or we'll be late,' I said.

'Why don't you stay the night?' he asked.

'We can't because the plane must have set off to fetch us already,' I responded very firmly.

We packed into the truck. As we rumbled along Colin said, 'I'll show you where I'm going to end up.' He drove a bit further and stopped in front of a collapsed looking wooden building of two stories, with a long veranda. On this were sitting an assortment of aged black people: men and women in broken deck chairs.

'That's the old peoples' home,' he said cheerfully.

The way back seemed quicker and smoother than in the morning. Perhaps Colin took a different road. We kissed him goodbye and I felt rather a pang at his evident loneliness. I thought of the grandeur of the old days. As the little plane lifted off the ground I felt a tremendous sense of relief and started looking forward to the white beach in the morning.

ELEVEN

Petersham

I was still pretty depressed on the whole, whilst living at Biddestone and so my doctor suggested that I should become a magistrate. I had some interviews and was accepted. It was an extremely interesting job and I learnt a good deal about life. I sat on the bench for seven years and occasionally took the chair, which you could after four years' experience. I found that quite nerve-racking and sometimes would sit alone at weekends if there were emergency cases. It was often pretty grisly.

One day my son Konrad told us about the most perfect house that belonged to a friend of his, an Austrian lady that we knew slightly. He described it as a house fit for a retired king. At around the same time I went to a dinner given by my friend, Annabel Goldsmith, who has a magical home in Ham. It was for Jack Lemmon, the actor. It was a wonderfully hot night and we sat in the garden at round tables.

On the way back, as I was being driven home, I could see all the lovely old houses. I passed Rutland Lodge, a grand early eighteenth century house with high gates – and also Montrose House opposite. I thought to myself that if we lived in this eighteenth century suburb, then we wouldn't have to go away at weekends and would be only twenty five minutes drive from central London.

Konrad asked me if I would like to meet his friend and see the house, which also happened to be in Petersham. It was called Petersham Lodge and wasn't for sale at that time. We went for tea. Once I had laid my eyes on it I fell totally in love with it. It was, and is, the perfect house for when the children are grown up and departed on their life pilgrimages. I had a sleepless night with my heart pounding. I knew I had to have the house. I knew that it was meant to be.

Some time elapsed in which I wrote to the owner and said that if ever she wanted to sell to please let me know first. Rupert did not know what I was planning. After about a year the house went on the market and I told him we had to sell Biddestone and move to Richmond. He was horrified and dead set against

Above: A view from Richmond Hill, painted by William Westall (1781-1850).
A present from Rupert.

Opposite page: Petersham Lodge from the garden and a photograph by Laurence Hill of the
view of Petersham Lodge and the meadow, taken from Richmond Hill.

the plan. In the end however I managed to persuade him. We sold Biddestone
well and quickly due to our great friend, Gerald Harford, a brilliant estate agent.
So all was set.

We bought the house, but lo' and behold we found that it was riddled with dry
rot. I felt so guilty, as obviously it cost a fortune to replace the rotten timbers.
This took a year. But my husband was wonderfully tolerant and patient. I
enjoyed decorating the house no end. It was one of the happiest times in my life.
We moved in in about 1989. My mother was still alive and greatly disapproved
of the move, preferring us to stay in the country as she had got attached to
Biddestone, as had Dora. I couldn't wait to get away and I have never looked
back.

My mother came round to see the new house.

'Well,' she said, 'it's certainly a handsome house, but why you want a huge,
great place like this I don't know.'

In fact it is much smaller than it looks and has three big rooms with high
ceilings on the ground floor and a good hall. Upstairs there are two good sized
bedrooms, an attic type room and two smaller other ones. It was just right in
every way. I got in touch with my dear friend, Lynette Hood, from Bath, to help

Dora and Manfredi on their wedding day with (left to right) Gaddo and Sibilla della
Gherardesca and Rudolf and Konrad.

with the decorating. We were thrilled with the results. We always got on well
and have very much the same taste.

When my bedroom was done my mother, on seeing it, said with a sniff, 'Well
it looks more like a drawing room.'

A friend of ours once said that as you get older you spend more time in the
bedroom and so you should make it look more like a drawing room. I think this
is very sensible.

* * *

In 1998, the time came for us to arrange Dora's wedding to Manfredi della
Gherardesca.

Dora wanted a small and quiet wedding. When she announced this to her
father, he said nothing. Instead he set about immediately planning what was
probably one of the last great, traditional Catholic weddings in Europe.

We had the most enormous Latin Nupital Mass and a congregation of over
nine hundred at the Brompton Oratory; the service took over two and a half

Top: Dora handing 'la busta' to Cardinal Poggi.
Above: Cardinal Poggi arriving in his cappa magna.

hours and there were fourteen pages and bridesmaids. Cardinal Poggi, head of the Vatican Library, presided and entered the Oratory wearing the cappa magna, which is seldom used now. Cardinal Poggi came over from Rome with his nephew, who was even smaller than him. We put them up in the Rembrandt Hotel, opposite the Oratory. On the day of the wedding, we produced the 'busta' to Poggi, to compensate him for his services. He carefully counted the money on the table and indicated that he was both pleased and satisfied with it. It reminded

With Mick Jagger before Dora's wedding.

me of that lunch in the palazzo in Rome all those years ago.

Rupert was in his element organizing the wedding and it was wonderful to see him so happy. He was like a general at the head of a military operation and attended to every detail. We had a reception afterwards at Petersham and the guests travelled from the Mass by bus. They were supplied with champagne en route.

* * *

With the passage of time, the doctor seems increasingly present. My own doctor is as smart as a magpie and usually wears a blue and white pinstriped suit. He is slim and has sleekly brushed dark hair. He often has a jaunty carnation in his buttonhole. He is a brilliant diagnostician and his many patients, including myself, feel that he has healing hands.

I once sat in front of him, before an antique kneehole desk. It had one or two small ornaments to one side and a jar of Smarties to give to younger patients. He placed my medical file in front of him and opened it. He seemed engrossed. I waited, my chest wheezing and aches and pains all over.

'I believe you know so and so?' he said, naming some friends in common.

'Oh yes,' I replied enthusiastically, 'they are such a nice couple, and have a beautiful house near ours.'

Then we embarked on a conversation about every aspect of the couple's life. He had met them on his holiday, he told me. At long last he motioned me to the bed, to be examined. By that time he was enquiring about the hunt that my daughter went out with.

'How is your glorious daughter?' he asked, adding, 'she is my all time favourite.'

This doctor had three daughters and a great many difficulties were discussed including unsuitable boyfriends. He finally rose and opened the door. As I walked towards it, I asked him whether he thought that I had bronchitis or not.

'Oh, yes,' he replied, 'your breathing is certainly sounding pretty old fashioned. That reminds me, I'll pop and get you something for it.'

'I've lost my sense of taste and smell for some time now,' I said to him.

'Nothing we can do about that I'm afraid,' he responded briskly.

He went into the dispensary across the passage and came back with a bottle of brightly coloured antibiotics.

'Take two of these three times a day. And don't overdo things!' he said cheerfully.

'Should I go to bed?' I asked, feeling pretty terrible by this point.

'Good God no, I shouldn't think so. Got a temperature?'

'Well, I don't think so, but my thermometer is broken.'

'Well be sure to give your wonderful daughter my love,' he replied gaily.

He saw me out to the door and stood breathing deeply for a moment on the step in the sunshine.

'It's awful being cooped up in there all day,' he said laughing, 'but I must get back to work now, as my secretary is at Ascot!'

* * *

I got into the car and my Irish daily of many years, called Mary, got into the front seat. Maxwell, a black and tan dachshund, jumped on to her lap. We whirled along on our way to Mr André, the vet. Max sat upright and kept a bright brown eye on the pavement to see if he could spot any dogs to bark at.

We parked in a side street by the surgery. Mary had him on the lead and as we got to the glass panelled front door he stopped dead, his four feet fixed firmly to the ground.

'Now be a good boy,' we both said to him, 'come along, it will be alright.'

He was heavy but we managed to lift him into the doorway. We sat down on a long banquette; at the other end was a nervous lady with a large box on her lap with two holes in it. A frantic pair of eyes stared out, immobile with fear. A small schoolboy sat next to her with his hamster in a cage.

The place was spotless and painted white. There was a counter at the end of the waiting room with two pleasant and pretty girls behind it with an appointment book in front of them and rows of various medicines and sprays on shelves behind them.

'Well, how is Mugsy?' the blonde girl said.

'He does have a shiny coat doesn't he! What a lovely boy he is.'

(His name had been misspelt due to my Portuguese manservant's pronunciation of it. He usually brought him in).

Maxwell gave a low growl and strained forward, as he had spotted the cat's eyes. His hair rose in a line down his back.

A huge Alsatian entered with a rough looking man in jeans. Maxwell wrenched free and flew towards it. There was a squall, but somehow, with the skilful help of the lovely assistants, calm was restored.

'You should keep your pooch under control,' said the man wearing jeans, in rather a nasty tone. I thought that it was wiser not to reply.

The door opened and there was Mr André. He was dressed in a snowy overall. He was extremely cultivated, quiet and intelligent.

'Maxwell please,' he said.

'I think my doctor ought to wear an overall like that,' I thought, thinking of the magpie.

The assistant, with the help of Mary, lifted the little hound on to the examining table. He neatly bit the blonde's wrist.

'Oh dear, you are a fierce boy,' she said laughing.

Blood flowed from the wound.

'That's nothing,' she said.

'Better get a plaster Gloria,' said Mr André.

'I think we should put a muzzle on him,' I said anxiously. So they did. He struggled violently and had to have three people to hold him down, as he was abnormally strong. At last it was all over.

He toddled up the street for a calming little walk with Mary before getting into the car. He sat with his head on her chest, gazing into her eyes as if to tell her what a terrible time he'd been through.

'Yes, you're my lovely baby,' she said, over and over again, stroking him tenderly.

* * *

I sat in the waiting room. Through the open door was a hospital worker sneezing and coughing violently and retching into a handkerchief.

I was to have a hysterectomy. Arabs flowed up and down the passages. In the room opposite mine there were at least ten women sitting round in a circle, chattering like magpies with their television on at full blast and the door permanently open.

I warned the anaesthetist several times about the pills I was taking in case they didn't mix well with the anaesthetic. He appeared to be listening.

The operation was scheduled for seven o'clock in the morning. I only came around at around at seven o'clock that evening and for the first hour I could not see. My husband had been telephoning all day, but the nurses had made some excuse every time.

Later in the evening I found my elbows were sore and bleeding. I told the nurse, but she was not at all surprised. 'I'll just get some plasters for you,' she said. As I had been pushed along the corridors I suppose my elbows had scraped the walls.

* * *

I was admitted into supposedly one of the best hospitals in London. Sitting in the waiting room a poor child was being sick into the waste paper basket.

After being shown to my room a Chinese nurse appeared, smiling and bowing. She barely spoke English and I doubted whether she would have been able to cope in an emergency. She put a photograph of herself on my bedside table and explained a few things which were totally incomprehensible. And then she disappeared. My glaucoma operation was a success. When my dressings had to come off there was no room available for this. So a little table and chair was set up in the corridor for my specialist. He ripped off the plasters on my eye with no warning. I cried out.

'Keep still,' he said furiously.

I ordered a croissant for my breakfast. It arrived in a cloudy plastic cover and was virtually inedible. It tasted of damp cardboard. With my good eye I read that it was three months out of date. Perhaps they were relying on the patients not being able to read!

Having been made to put my purse into a safe downstairs on arrival, I was unable to retrieve it, due to the office having closed.

On reaching home I developed a severe intestinal infection which took some time to recover from. My surgeon also caught it and had to take several days off work, which had never happened before!

* * *

My beloved long haired dachshund was once savaged by a huge dog. The wounds seemed to heal but broke open again. Our vet recommended 'The Queen Mother's Hospital for Small Animals', just outside London. I had taken my Alsatian to be treated and eventually to be put to sleep there, and it had been excellent.

We filled out all of the forms at home. They had sent us an explanatory letter and a parking permit, all on crested paper. Questions on the forms were on breed, appearance, temperament, characteristics, diet, favourite food, flavours and meal times.

The waiting room was large and comfortable with a wallpaper design of dogs' paws.

Our surgeon and two assistants arrived in white coats and name badges. We were taken into a spotless and adequately sized consulting room. The surgeon apologised for what he described as, 'rather a small room.' He said that a better one would soon be available.

We soon transferred to an enormous airy room with an examination table in the middle, where my dog was gently laid. We had to leave her there for a week. She had her own personal nurse, a young man of great gentleness. He telephoned me twice a day throughout the week telling me every detail of her progress and even about her strolls in the garden. He said she was a lovely little dog and that he would miss her very much.

* * *

I had an appointment in London. It had been snowing and was icy underfoot. I stood in the hall, my dachshund Max glaring hypnotically at me. I hadn't had time to take him for his walk.

I was tired and strung up and had just had a strong coffee. 'Oh come on,' I said to him, 'let's go, but only for twenty minutes.' I did not bother to change my shoes, which were leather moccasins with slippery soles.

We went along the towpath and turned into the meadow below Richmond Hill. The path was covered with ice, so I went up a bit of a steep hill to avoid it. I suddenly slipped and my foot went into an unseen hole. My leg buckled over, shattering my ankle. I then fell on my elbow, shattering that too. The shock and pain were beyond description. I looked around and there was not a soul in sight. I waited and waited. Then, in the far distance I saw two women. I started to shout as loud as possible but they could not hear. At last, as they progressed along the towpath they stopped, looking slowly in all directions. It seemed so long before they suddenly saw me. They seemed rather timid and did not react very quickly, so I kept yelling. At last they got to me. They were a rather tentative mother and daughter. I told them that I was badly injured and, since this was before mobile phones, asked them if they could they go to a nearby pub to ring my home and 999. This they kindly did.

The ambulance arrived fairly soon afterwards. Then, as the paramedics approached, my dachshund, who was a fierce character, went for them and they rapidly backed off.

'Well we can't do anything for you if you don't get rid of that dog,' they said. Luckily our cook, Jacky, arrived from home and put him on his lead and also somehow got me into a sitting position. The medics were pretty hopeless and I had to get them to strap my arm, which was completely shattered, and hanging down my side, for the journey. We got to Kingston A&E and many hours later I got my X-rays. Luckily I was on BUPA, and luckier still, the private wing at Kingston had just been finished. They put me in a nice room just in front of the nursing centre. I had two major operations and was there for the best part of six weeks. The food was excellent and so was the nursing. At the end of my stay I got an infection or allergy over my whole body, I'm sure due to heavy doses of antibiotics, which I tried to refuse. I had several journeys down to X-ray, some of them somewhat hazardous. Many kind friends came to visit, among them my friend Annabel Goldsmith. At that point I was allowed to sit in the chair for a while. She had a bad back so lay on my bed. She then pulled all the surgical gloves out of a container in the wall.

I asked her why.

'They're so useful for bathing the dogs!' she replied.

On returning home I was told that I had to spend another six weeks in bed and that I was not allowed to be carried downstairs either, only by ambulance men when I had to go to X-ray.

It was a grim time but I met so many wonderful nurses and my surgeon could not have been more expert and kind.

I managed to keep up my piano by playing on my upright with my left arm propped on a table. Many kind friends visited and often had meals in my room.

*　　*　　*

Rudolf, after having taught for a long time in a comprehensive school, decided to go into the church. He became a Dominican. My heart was seared and was

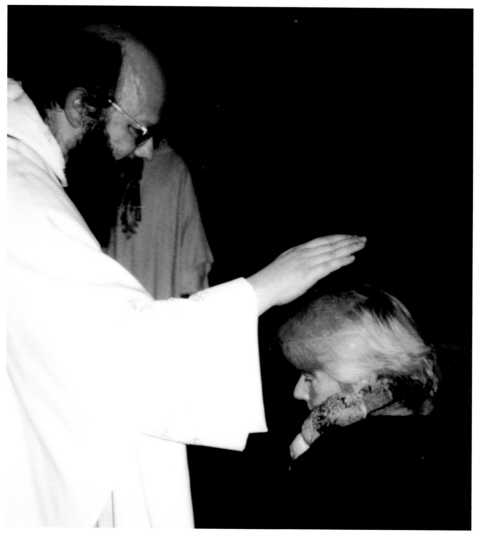

Rudolf blessing me at the end of his ordination at the Dominican Priory in North London.

Rudolf and Rupert resting during my seventy fifth birthday party.

searing. I was driving to Rudolf's house, which backed onto the river on the outskirts of London. It was a lovely house, quite ordinary really: immaculate and at the same time homely. He had three quiet intellectual lodgers: a chirpy young schoolmaster, a reliable spotty girl and a rather sinister looking other, who was a gardener.

I was a bit early, just in case. We sat in the kitchen while he ate his breakfast of muesli and cream cake.

Rudolf was tall, fair and slightly balding. He had very direct and clear blue eyes and regular features. He possessed a depth of penetrating gaze that reminded me of those ancient Russian icons.

He carefully washed up and replaced the dishes on his own special shelf. I wondered whenever they would be used again and admired the tiny garden through the glass door of the kitchen. It was stuffed with flowers, so much so, that there was no room to walk or sit in it; but they never wanted to anyway, nor did they have time.

One of the lodgers hovered about smiling through his heavy horn rim glasses, pleased at my compliments about the garden, which he tended in his spare time in lieu of a lower rent. He was dressed in a strange conglomeration of clothes, of the sort that we used to throw on for the air raid shelter in the war.

When the lodger had gone upstairs we sat together and my heart seared again. 'Oh,' I thought, 'he is my most beloved son, and it will never be the same. How could he leave all this?'

He was going to Scotland to begin his novitiate to join the Dominican Order of Friars. The first stretch would be nine months. He had only recently returned from Russia and a hard postulancy in tough conditions. Trials consisted of having no hot water and sometimes no water at all. Since he did not like dogs he was made to look after an untrained mongrel. He had to do mountains of washing up and spend hours scraping paint off windows with a knife. The superior had also taken a dislike to him.

'We'd better go,' I said.

The lodgers helped to load the car. The cats sat looking on detachedly, sitting upright with their paws placed tightly together like little cushions. My son said goodbye warmly and briefly to his friends and kissed the spotty girl.

As we drove along I glanced at Rudolf in the car to see if there was any trace of sadness or regret. There was none – perhaps just a trace of nostalgia.

'I really love London you know,' he said in his slow and deliberate voice. 'Look at all those familiar old buildings, all of them remind me of something.'

He looked out of the window.

I had always known there was something special about him. He was born prematurely and had jaundice and I always thought that he was hovering between life and death. He was very pale and weak and slept a lot. Only when he was born had I started to believe in God. I had converted to Catholicism a few months before.

I remembered feeling that he had a Holy atmosphere or aura about him. I felt this on and off when I was with him and sometimes it came to me after he had left me. It still does.

He had been mulling over going into the Church for many years during which time he had led a hard life teaching in a comprehensive school. I had worried about him greatly as it was about the roughest, and toughest, job to have, especially in the district where he taught. He was determined and also extremely interested in the job – but I felt it was somewhat of an endurance test.

At that time, we lived in a flat in Kensington. Rudolf had to get up very early and sometimes he would eat his breakfast in the dark before going to work. Then, I always knew he was very depressed. Later he was much better, when he moved to the house on the river and made new friends.

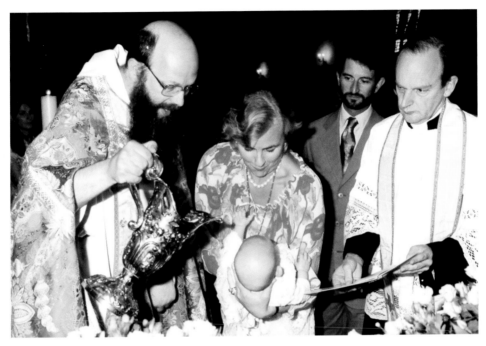

Rudolf, Dora, Manfredi and Konrad at the christening of Margherita in Castagneto.

We swept along towards King's Cross only too quickly.

Luckily when we got there we found a bay for the car with no nagging metre attendant in sight. A car load of Indians came alongside and looked closely at us.

Rudolf perched on the back of the open station wagon and put on his backpack and loaded himself all over with bags.

'Well, goodbye then,' he said. 'Thanks for the lift.'

He kissed me briefly.

'It was lucky I thought of it,' I said.

(I had been upset because for some reason I had not thought of driving him to the station before. 'I didn't think of it either,' he had said.)

He walked away towards the entrance of the teeming station. He was to meet his brother at the ticket office.

I watched his figure until it disappeared. Despair came over me.

'It's like a death,' I thought in my heart. 'Everything is given up, rejected. No, I must not think of it like that, it is what he wants, and if it makes him happy it must be right.'

I drove away into the eternal traffic jams again. My eyes filled with tears. I felt drained and empty and always my heart seared.

Margherita and Aliotto as page and bridesmaid to Prince and
Princess Charles-Philippe d'Orléans.

Princess Michael of Kent with my grandson Aliotto at a lunch during
our golden wedding celebrations in Italy.

Six days later Rudolf rang. Everything was going well. 'My correct title is
Brother now,' he said gravely. The food was good, he told me – it was warm,
and he liked all the others.

At that time I knew a charming old gentleman, an immigrant from wartime
whose wife had died some years before, and almost directly after this his only
daughter had become an enclosed nun. He came to lunch and we wandered
around the chilly garden together discussing what it was like.

I said the bit about death to him. 'Oh yes,' he said 'why sometimes it gives me
a shock when I realise I have not thought about Marie for a week, but as I can
have no contact with her it is inevitable that a healing process begins with time,
as in bereavement.'

He was a very kind and compassionate man and had suffered greatly in his
life, also lately enduring a heart by-pass operation. He had not told his daughter
about it until afterwards.

'How brave he is,' I thought. But of course the likes of his daughter and my
son did not distinguish too much between life and death. At least I felt honoured
and privileged to have such a son.

The family line up at my seventy-fifth birthday party.

An old friend of mine, a devout Catholic, who had six sons, wrote saying, 'My goodness you are lucky having a Dominican son!' Rudolf was thrilled by this letter and laughed a lot.

After Christmas Rudolf was allowed to leave the monastery for five nights. He came to see us, or rather spared us one dinner! He had so many friends and interests that his time was carefully divided between them all.

He looked magnificent in his white robe and black cowl. He had a leather belt with a rosary hanging from it. I thought he looked like an El Greco painting. He had a very calm and slightly severe aura.

I felt that he was happy.

* * *

In 2014, Rupert died, after a long battle with illness. I miss his kindness and wise counsel and will never forget his wit and storytelling, always in different languages. He was, I think, a really remarkable man: he certainly succeeded and

With Aliotto at Eton for his confirmation.

Margherita and Aliotto at the celebrations for Dora's fiftieth birthday

was exceptionally generous to all around him, including his family, his friends and his employees. But he was also deeply religious and scrupulously honest: intellectual, highly educated and well read. Like many clever people, he was interested in everyone and everything around him. He had a passionate interest and knowledge of classical music and was much bemused by the pop world that he became involved with.

My children meanwhile, have followed different, but equally interesting paths.

Both of my sons are priests. Rudolf continues to teach in a school near to the Dominican Priory in North London, of which he is a member. He is a brilliant teacher and could, I think, teach anybody anything. He plays several instruments, is a talented linguist and crochets the most beautiful rugs and bedcovers in his spare time. Konrad is also a Catholic priest and has been in Venice for about twelve years. For a while he ran a church there called S. Simone Piccolo. He says the Old Latin Rite, to which he is devoted, and enjoys arranging the music and looking after his parishioners. He hears confessions in San Marco in several languages. For a while he lived on a mountaintop on my son-in-law's estate in Italy, but now he is back in Venice. He is a talented writer and pianist and a brilliant and convincing mimic.

My daughter Dora, always capable and outgoing as a girl, has taken after her father and inherited his good business brain. She is a keen rider and devotes a lot of her time to riding, hunting and eventing. She has run an entertainment business for big events for many years and now she manages Rupert's business, which she took over when he died. She is the best daughter anyone could have and, like both her brothers, she is a constant and devoted support to me.

But now my life is in Petersham. It is my dream house, with my dream garden. I love every minute that I spend here and long to get back, even when I am out for a short time or away on holiday. I am lucky to have the most wonderful people here to help me run the house and garden. I have also been on the Petersham Trust for many years. Chris Brasher, the Olympic runner, founded this with a large endowment, to protect the twenty-five acre meadow and view from Richmond Hill for posterity.

It was thanks to Konrad that I discovered Petersham Lodge. My two grandchildren were born whilst we were here – Aliotto (an ancient della Gherardesca name) is now sixteen and Margherita is fourteen – and my own children still often come to stay. And then there are my beloved dogs!

Long may it last.

Florence and Beau at Petersham Lodge.

'All knowledge, the totality of all questions and all answers
is contained in the dog.'
FRANZ KAFKA

Acknowledgements

I am much indebted to Hugo Vickers for all his help and encouragement; to Laurence Hill for photography and countless other vital work; to Elizabeth Vickers for photography; and to Sally Renny for organising my book launch. I would also like to thank our secretary, Dee Anstice, who has been with my husband and me for thirty happy years, for all of her hard work.

Finally, I could not have achieved this book without my brilliant young editor, Tom Perrin. A thousand thanks to all!

I am grateful to the following for giving me permission to use illustrations for which they hold the copyright: Lord Snowdon, the frontispiece; Reinaldo Herrera, page 93, Alice Kadel, page 114; Michael Dillon, page 138; The Mustique Company, page 157; Laurence Hill, pages 171, 190; James Yeats-Brown, page 189.

Index